Executive Summary

This report summarises the main findings from the survey element of the project to map provision for students with learning difficulties and/or disabilities.

Introduction and background (Chapter 1)

The survey element of the mapping project reported here had the following objectives:

- to provide estimates of the level and nature of participation by people with learning difficulties and/or disabilities in further education;

- to provide a baseline of information about the numbers and characteristics of students with learning difficulties and/or disabilities, which can be monitored in future years through the individualised student record (ISR);

- to make some preliminary estimates (in the absence of a comprehensive population/household survey) of the nature and scale of 'unmet need' for further education among students with learning difficulties and/or disabilities.

A pilot interview study was undertaken in 20 further education establishments in late spring 1995, and a postal questionnaire was piloted with a sample of 100 sector colleges in the summer term of 1995. The main survey was launched in October 1995, covering all sector colleges and a sample of external institutions. The survey related to all students enrolled on 1 November 1995, and was closed in mid-March 1996 with a response rate of just over 60% (274 colleges).

The distribution of responses by type of college and region (see map on p.iv) is statistically representative of the sector as a whole, but higher response rates were achieved from larger institutions.

Students with learning difficulties and/or disabilities (Chapter 2)

Numbers of students

Across 272 colleges providing full data, 81,892 students are identified as having a learning difficulty and/or disability. Grossing this up to a national level implies that, for the further education sector as a whole in England, there are some 126,500 students with learning difficulties and/or disabilities which represents between 5.3% and 5.7% of the enrolled student population in November 1995[1].

Similar shares of students with learning difficulties and/or disabilities are reported in all the main college types, with the exception that a higher share (8.2%) is reported in agriculture and horticulture colleges, and a much lower share (1.4%) is found in the small number of specialist designated institutions.

Generally, the proportion of students identified as having learning difficulties and/or disabilities tends to decrease with college size, although it rises again in the largest size group (colleges with 10,000 students or more).

The proportion of students identified as having learning difficulties and/or disabilities varies between regions (from 3.4% in the Greater London region to 7.8% in the Northern Region). This variation is not explicable simply in terms of different regions having different balances of large and small colleges, although the balance of college types between regions does appear to have an influence.

Characteristics of students

Just under 50% of the students with learning difficulties and/or disabilities are female; a slight under-representation compared with female students in the overall enrolled student population.

Over 55% of students with learning difficulties and/or disabilities attend part time. This is also a lower share than is found in the overall student population. Female students are more likely to study part time than are male students.

The mode of attendance varies according to the type of college, with sixth form colleges in particular having very few part-time students with learning difficulties and/or disabilities. In all college types, the share of students with learning difficulties and/or disabilities who are part time is lower than the share of part-timers among the corresponding overall student population.

Regional patterns reflect the balance of college types with the South East region for example having the highest share of sixth form colleges and the lowest share of students with learning difficulties and/or disabilities.

The age distribution of students with learning difficulties and/or disabilities is similar to that for all students, with some 33% of students aged 16 to 18, and 50% aged 25 or older. A much higher proportion of older students are part time.

A higher proportion (80%) of students with learning difficulties and/or disabilities record their ethnic origin as 'white' than for the student population as a whole. Regional variations in this proportion are broadly consistent with variations in the overall ethnic minority population.

Learning programmes followed

Just over 50% of students with learning difficulties and/or disabilities are studying on integrated provision, with just under half studying on programmes designed solely or primarily for students with learning difficulties and/or disabilities ('discrete provision'). A much higher proportion of part-time than full-time students are attending discrete programmes.

Nearly 50% of the students with learning difficulties and/or disabilities are studying on pre-vocational or foundation courses (that is, pre-(G)NVQ level 1). Only 16% are following programmes at level 3 or above (this contrasts with the 41% of all enrolled students following programmes at level 3 or above).

Identification of students with learning difficulties and/or disabilities

Over 90% of colleges attempt to identify full-time students with a learning difficulty and/or disability irrespective of whether they need learning support; around 30% do not extend this approach to part-time students. There are variations between college types and sizes in this approach (smaller colleges in general and sixth form colleges, in particular, being less likely to identify all students, irrespective of learning support needs).

Despite this approach, a significant minority (nearly 50%) of colleges believe that they may have enrolled students with learning difficulties and/or disabilities who have not been formally identified, and among those prepared to estimate the size of this group, the average number of such students was assessed to be more than 50 in each college.

Nature of learning difficulties and/or disabilities and learning support received (Chapter 3)

Nature of learning difficulties and/or disabilities

In the description of learning difficulties, 19% of students with learning difficulties and/or disabilities are described as having moderate learning difficulties, 15% as having severe

371:19

·hɔr

Mapping
Provision

● ●

Prepared by

The Institute for Employment Studies

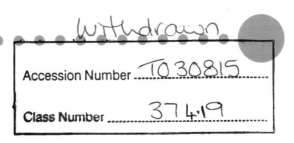

CONTENTS

FEFC Regions

Northern
Region

North
West

Yorkshire &
Humberside

East
Midlands

West
Midlands

Eastern
Region

Greater
London

South
East

South
West

learning difficulties, and a further 9% as having specific learning difficulties (such as dyslexia). The remainder have a wide range of different disabilities and/or learning difficulties.

Sixth form colleges stand out as having much lower than average proportions of students with moderate and (especially) severe learning difficulties, and much higher than average proportions of students with specific learning difficulties, among their students with learning difficulties and/or disabilities.

Larger colleges tend to have a higher proportion of students with severe learning difficulties, students with multiple or profound disabilities, and students with mental illness, and lower proportions of students with specific learning difficulties.

Learning support provided

A wide range of learning support provision is offered by colleges. Most common are:

- support assistants (non-teaching), and supplementary teaching (outside main course), both of which are found in between 70% and 80% of colleges;

- specialist equipment; specialist assessment; communicators and specialist teaching for hearing-impaired students; and drop-in support centres; each are found in between 60% and 70% of colleges.

Virtually all types of learning support provision are more widespread in general further education colleges and tertiary colleges than in sixth form colleges, art and design or agriculture and horticulture colleges. Similarly, the incidence of most types of learning support increases with college size.

Cost of and funding for learning support (Chapter 3 (part) and Chapter 4)

Nearly 66% of students with a learning difficulty and/or disability are identified as receiving learning support, and over 70% of these students receive learning support which is wholly or partly funded by the FEFC.

Whether such support is wholly or partly FEFC-funded varies considerably according to the nature of the support. Thus only 10% of colleges report that social work support is FEFC-funded, whilst at the other extreme 91% of colleges report that non-teaching support assistants are FEFC-funded.

Among the 189 colleges providing the relevant data, 45% of students who receive funding through the FEFC additional support bands receive it for reasons not associated with a learning difficulty and/or disability, but for some other reason (such as a literacy, numeracy, or English as a second or other language (ESOL) need).

Where learning support for students with learning difficulties and/or disabilities is funded through the FEFC's additional support bands, nearly 75% of students fall within band 0 (£170–£500 annual cost for each student), band 1 (£501–£1,000) or band 2 (£1,001–£2,000). Sixth form colleges, and art and design colleges record higher than average proportions of students in these lower bands.

Some 66% of colleges report that some of their students with learning difficulties and/or disabilities receive learning support wholly or partially funded through non-FEFC sources. Sixth form colleges are the least reliant on non-FEFC sources for learning support funding.

The main sources of non-FEFC funding for additional learning support are colleges' own internal budgets[2] (used in 60% of cases), and the local education authority (LEA) (49%).

3

Mapping Provision: The Provision of and Participation in Further Education by Students with Learning Difficulties and/or Disabilities

Unmet need (Chapter 5)

Internal unmet need

The survey revealed that 30% of colleges report that there are enrolled students who have been identified as having a learning support need which the college cannot meet. There are on average 30 such students in each one of those colleges (56) which are able to estimate the number of students affected.

These unmet needs among already enrolled students arise from a wide range of sources, most common being basic skills or ESOL needs, or needs arising from dyslexia or visual impairment.

Staffing constraints, followed by physical resource constraints (often associated with specialist equipment, or physical access issues) are most often cited as the reasons for the college's being unable to meet the needs of enrolled students with learning difficulties and/or disabilities.

External unmet need

Just under 66% of colleges have systems in place to record instances where potential students with a learning difficulty and/or disability apply to the institution but cannot be enrolled. There had been (in the year to date at the time of the survey) an average of 3.9 such students in each college among those 150 colleges able to make an estimate of the number of students affected.

The needs which cannot be met and which have led to potential students being 'turned away' vary, but common examples include students requiring support such as transport, 24-hour or residential care, continuous or frequent personal care. Disabilities affecting mobility top the list of specific disability types whose needs colleges report they cannot meet in this context, followed by profound and/or complex disabilities.

Of those colleges identifying external unmet need, less than 50% feel that such needs are being met by other local providers.

Nearly 66% of colleges report having systems in place for identifying unexpressed demand for further education among people who have a learning difficulty and/or disability in the local population. This is higher than expected. Those colleges (77) able to make an estimate suggested that there are on average over 300 such potential students for each college.

For the most part, however, such estimates are generally based on informal, unsystematic information gathering, and are heavily dependent on local institutional networks (such as with schools, the careers service, social and health services). Few colleges have in place any systematic or comprehensive data gathering or analysis of local population and demographic factors to inform this process.

Colleges' overall approach to provision for students with learning difficulties and/or disabilities (Chapter 6)

When asked, most colleges report a strategic approach to provision for students with learning difficulties and/or disabilities which is 'inclusive', based on principles of open access, with cross-institution learning support provision and widespread assessment of most or all students.

There is some correlation between the overall approach to provision in this sense, and the proportion of a college's enrolled students who are identified as having learning difficulties and/or disabilities.

ENDNOTES

1 More precise estimates are not possible, however, until the full data set from the November 1995 ISR becomes available.

2 Clearly, a significant proportion of funding identified as coming from 'internal college budgets' will have originated from the FEFC via the recurrent funding methodology. The point here is that this was not covered by FEFC funding specifically allocated for additional learning support (for example, through the additional support bands).

5

Mapping Provision: The Provision of and Participation in Further Education by Students with Learning Difficulties and/or Disabilities

Introduction and Background

Research objectives

1   This report sets out the main findings of a research project undertaken by the Institute for Employment Studies (IES) on behalf of the learning difficulties and/or disabilities committee of the Further Education Funding Council (FEFC or the Council). The object of the project was to map the provision of and participation in further education by people with learning difficulties and/or disabilities.

2   At a more detailed level, the project had four inter-related objectives, each corresponding to a distinct part of the project:

Part A: to estimate the incidence of learning difficulties and/or disabilities in the post-16 population on the basis of existing demographic and secondary data. This part was conducted internally by FEFC staff. The research findings are summarised in appendix 3;

Part B: to estimate the numbers and characteristics of students with learning difficulties and/or disabilities participating in further education. This part of the study was undertaken by IES and was conducted in two stages:

– stage 1: this was concerned with assessing the feasibility of making estimates of participation on the basis of existing information available to the FEFC, and making recommendations for further primary survey work in stage 2 of the project;

– stage 2: following our recommendations in stage 1, this stage consisted of a survey of further education institutions to collect data necessary to make the participation estimates required by the committee and the FEFC;

Part C: to assess the factors influencing participation and non-participation in further education by people with learning difficulties and/or disabilities. This part of the study was also divided into two stages:

– stage 1: this examined the factors influencing participation, drawing on existing information, and made recommendations for further primary research to supplement and fill gaps in this latter information;

– stage 2: this was planned to consist of the primary research recommended in stage 1. At the time of writing, however, it has yet to be decided, whether, and in what precise form, this supplementary primary research is to be conducted;

Part D: to estimate the level of unmet need, that is, the number of people aged 16 and over with learning difficulties and/or disabilities wishing to participate in further education, but who cannot or do not currently do so. It was agreed, however, at an early stage of the research, that without a full-scale representative survey of people with learning difficulties and/or disabilities in the population, it would not be possible to meet in full this part of the FEFC's brief for the research. Some, more limited, steps towards estimating unmet need were, however, judged to be feasible through the college survey conducted for part B of the research, and the relevant findings are reported in chapter 5.

Rationale and design of the college survey

3   The central methodology for the parts of the research reported here (part B, stage 2 and part D), therefore, was a survey of

providers (colleges), which aims to build on the preliminary work undertaken in stage 1 of the study in order to:

- provide estimates of the level and nature of participation by people with learning difficulties and/or disabilities in further education;

- provide a comprehensive baseline of information on participation which can be monitored over time, and updated through the use of the individualised student record (ISR), and other sources as appropriate;

- make some preliminary estimates (in the absence of a comprehensive population/household survey) of the nature and scale of 'unmet need' for further education among people with learning difficulties and/or disabilities.

4   The survey of all colleges was deemed necessary because although the ISR goes a considerable way towards meeting the requirements of the Council and the committee, it was not originally designed to meet our requirements, and hence leaves a number of gaps in the data which can be filled only through survey-based research. In particular:

- the (self-assessed) disability fields in the ISR do not allow a distinction to be made between different types of learning difficulty and/or disability. This limits the comparisons that can be made with external population incidence data (identified in part A of the project), as well as making it impossible to meet the requirement specified in the original research brief that the research construct a full 'profile of students with learning difficulties and/or disabilities currently participating in further education', this profile to include information on 'type of disability';

- the ISR does not allow the possibility of matching this participation profile with the nature of provision offered by colleges, nor with a number of key variables identified in the original research brief (notably the 'forms of additional support, if any, offered by the college, including the provision of transport'). The ISR's scope in this respect is currently limited to the identification of the 'additional support band', if any, which applies to the student in question, under the Council's funding methodology. This causes (at least) three key difficulties for the present research:

– it does not identify additional support provided which either falls below the minimum threshold of the Council's banding structure, or which is funded from other (college or external) sources;

– it does not identify the nature of additional support provided, but only the cost range into which it falls;

– it covers individuals who may not have a learning difficulty and/or disability in the sense used by the Council, according to the *Further and Higher Education Act 1992*, but who are in receipt of additional learning support for other reasons (for example, because their first language is not English, or because they are receiving literacy or numeracy support, but do not otherwise have a learning difficulty and/or disability).

5   This implied that there was a need for a comprehensive survey of further education providers which should concentrate on supplementing the ISR database with:

- information on the types of learning difficulties and disabilities of students enrolled in the institution in question;

- information on whether and how these students have been assessed as requiring additional support;

- information on the nature and cost of support provided to these students (including non-FEFC-funded additional support).

6   In addition, it was felt that there would be value in collecting data in the survey on issues concerned with the college's overall approach to provision for students with learning difficulties and/or disabilities (such as 'inclusive' vs 'discrete' provision; existence of cross-institution learning support; co-ordinated approach to assessment). This would enable some analysis of whether different strategic approaches to provision for students with learning difficulties and/or disabilities were associated with different patterns and levels of participation.

7   Extensive piloting of the survey was undertaken, first through face-to-face interviews with a sample of 20 sector colleges, and second through a pilot postal survey of 100 colleges (chosen from those involved in the first phase of implementation of the ISR). The piloting was important in order to test a number of key design issues.

8   Firstly, there was an important choice to be made between data collection at the *individual student level* and at the *aggregate college level*. Our initial view was that the latter was to be preferred, subject to the pilot's confirming that this could be done in a way which allowed both a link with the ISR data aggregated to college level, and an examination of the relationships between types of learning difficulties and/or disabilities and the nature and level of additional support provided. The pilots confirmed that for the majority of colleges such an approach would be feasible.

9   Secondly, the feasibility of collecting comprehensive data on the characteristics of the learning difficulties and/or disabilities of individual students needed to be further tested. The first phase of the research suggested that this might be problematic in some colleges where the inclusive approach to provision is based on the identification of individual learning support needs rather than personal characteristics. It was important, therefore, to establish whether these colleges would be able and willing to provide such data, and whether their well-

founded concerns on this issue could be addressed when they fully understood the purpose of the research (without such data the study would be unable fully to meet its stated objectives). Again, piloting confirmed that the majority of colleges could provide aggregate data in the required format and would, in most cases, be prepared so to do.

10   Thirdly, whilst it was clear that most colleges could at least identify those students with learning difficulties and/or disabilities to whom they were providing additional learning support, the piloting was necessary to test how far it would be possible to identify and collect data on: a) those students with learning difficulties and/or disabilities who had not been identified as requiring additional learning support; and b) those who did not require such support. In order to be able to make overall participation estimates and comparisons with external population data, estimates of students in these latter two categories would be required. The piloting confirmed that it would not be possible to collect full data from all colleges on these two groups, but that a sufficient number of colleges could make estimates of the size of these groups for it to be worthwhile including such students in the data collection exercise[1].

11   Finally, the pilots examined how far colleges could go in making estimates of 'unmet need' among students and potential students with learning difficulties and/or disabilities. Our interest was both in 'internal' unmet need (that is, enrolled students whose needs could not fully be met), and 'external' unmet need (that is, potential students who could not be enrolled because their needs could not be met, or who were unlikely to apply for, or consider further education because of their learning difficulties and/or disabilities). Despite this being considered the most difficult topic on which to collect data, many of the pilot respondents were confident about being able to provide some information on these issues.

9

Mapping Provision: The Provision of and Participation in Further Education by Students with Learning Difficulties and/or Disabilities

The numbers might be inaccurate, it was commonly argued, but the general scale of internal and to some extent external unmet need was evident to a high proportion of college learning support co-ordinators. The extent to which such information formed part of college records varied, but it was judged feasible to include a limited range of questions on these issues in the final survey questionnaire (see appendix 2).

The survey

12   Following the pilot interview study conducted with further education institutions in late spring 1995, and the pilot postal questionnaire survey in summer 1995, a full survey of all 453 sector colleges and a sample of 50 external institutions[2] was launched in October 1995 ('external institutions' include those maintained by local education authorities and other institutions outside the sector offering FEFC-funded further education provision). The intention was that the survey should collect data referring to the position as at 1 November 1995 and, as far as possible, was designed to be consistent with the ISR, the current return for which also refers to 1 November 1995.

13   The original questionnaire asked colleges to send their completed returns to IES by 1 January 1996. In practice, only a minority of colleges were able to meet this requirement[3]. Following discussion with the FEFC, it was agreed to extend the deadline, given the importance of achieving as complete a return as possible from the survey.

14   The data presented in this report are based on returns which had been received at IES and coded for computer analysis by mid-March 1996. The data refer to 274 sector colleges responding (a response rate of just over 60%). In addition to the 274 sector colleges, responses were received from 31 external institutions (a response rate of 62%). The process of analysis was further complicated by the need, in many cases, to re-contact colleges which had submitted returns, in order to check and correct apparent inconsistencies in the data. Despite the extensive piloting, colleges faced inevitable difficulties in providing consistent data. These difficulties had their origins in a number of factors:

- colleges had adopted a variety of definitions and categorisations of different types of learning difficulties and/or disabilities, often not compatible with those being used in the survey;

- in some cases colleges did not record such data at all; the overall definition of learning difficulties and/or disabilities adopted by the committee (and incorporated in the survey), which excluded basic skills and/or ESOL needs, was problematic for a number of colleges;

- the survey did not collect data on total numbers and characteristics of all enrolled students — these data were collected in the pilot, but were excluded from the final survey on grounds that they would duplicate the ISR and thus constitute an unnecessary data collection burden on colleges.

Characteristics of responding colleges

15   The analysis is based on data from 274 sector colleges which had responded to the survey by mid-March 1996.

16   Table 1 shows that just over 50% of these respondents were general further education colleges, around 25% were sixth form colleges, a further 13% were tertiary colleges, and the rest were art and design, agriculture and horticulture colleges or specialist designated institutions. This distribution, although based on just over 60% of all sector colleges, is statistically representative of the distribution of college types in the overall sector college population, as shown in the final column of table 1. Similarly, the regional distribution of the 274

respondents (shown in table 2) broadly corresponds to that of the overall college population, although the match is less precise, with regional variations in response rates resulting in some regions (West Midlands, Yorkshire and Humberside and Eastern Region) being slightly over-represented, and others (South East, East Midlands and North West) slightly under-represented among respondents.

Table 3 examines the distribution of respondents by another key variable — size of institution, as defined by the number of students enrolled.

17 The initial intention was to include in the survey a range of questions about the entire enrolled student population in each college, with which to compare the corresponding data on students with learning difficulties and/or disabilities. Following the

Table 1.   Respondents by type of institution

Institution type	Respondents		Institution type/ sector (N = 453)
	No.	%	%
Agriculture and horticulture college	18	6.6	7.1
Art and design college	7	2.6	2.0
General further education college	140	51.1	48.8
Sixth form college	66	24.1	24.3
Specialist designated institution	7	2.6	3.3
Tertiary college	36	13.1	14.6
Total (N=100%)	**274**	**100.0**	**100.0**

Table 2.   Respondents by FEFC region

FEFC region	Respondents		Institution type/ sector (N = 453)
	No.	%	%
East Midlands	20	7.3	8.8
Eastern Region	28	10.2	8.6
Greater London	36	13.1	13.7
North West	35	12.8	15.0
Northern Region	15	5.5	6.2
South East	35	12.8	15.5
South West	26	9.5	9.1
West Midlands	45	16.4	13.2
Yorkshire and Humberside	34	12.4	9.9
Total (N=100%)	**274**	**100.0**	**100.0**

11

pilot, however, in the interests of reducing the burden of data provision on colleges, it was decided to drop these questions and to obtain these data from the relevant sections of the ISR returns. In the absence of 1995 ISR data, we have used total enrolments data from the corresponding point in the previous year (November 1994) provided to us by the FEFC.

18   Table 3 shows that the size distribution of our respondents is skewed towards larger colleges. In other words, there was a higher response rate to the survey from larger colleges. Thus, whilst the overall survey response rate was, as we have seen, just over 60%, this varied from 52% among the smallest colleges (with fewer than 1,000 students) to 84% among the largest (with 10,000 students or more). This means, on the one hand, that the survey's coverage of the overall student population is rather greater than that implied by the 60% survey response rate. On the other hand, it implies that care needs to be taken in generalising results from the survey to the population as a whole — specifically, any results which vary by college size must be appropriately weighted before they can be applied to the overall college population in England[4].

Structure and purpose of the report

19   The main function of the study was, as its title suggests, to gather information. The objective was to map, for the first time, the extent and nature of provision for and participation in further education by students with learning difficulties and/or disabilities in England. The study was explicitly not aimed at proffering explanations for, or opinions on, the patterns observed in the findings, and the authors have, therefore, refrained from putting forward such explanations and opinions in the report. The report is structured as follows:

* chapter 2 sets out the basic statistical findings on the numbers, distribution and characteristics of enrolled students with learning difficulties and/or disabilities across the sector; the types of learning programmes being followed by these students, and college approaches to the identification of students with learning difficulties and/or disabilities;

* in chapter 3 we look at the types of learning difficulties and/or disabilities recorded among enrolled students, and their incidence; as well as the nature of learning support these students receive;

Table 3.   Respondents by size of institution

Enrolled students	Respondents		Institution type/ sector (N = 453)
	No.	%	%
0–999	43	15.7	18.1
1,000–2,499	57	20.8	21.5
2,500–4,999	44	16.1	18.8
5,000–7,499	61	22.3	21.9
7,500–9,999	28	10.2	8.9
10,000 or more	41	15.0	10.8
Total (N=100%)	274	100.0	100.0

Note: college size as at November 1994

- chapter 4 examines how the provision of learning support for students with learning difficulties and/or disabilities was funded, and the role played by the FEFC's additional support arrangements/bands *vis à vis* other funding sources;

- chapter 5 explores the issue of 'unmet need' both in terms of the extent to which colleges could meet the needs of students with learning difficulties and/or disabilities *already enrolled*, and in terms of their ability to meet the needs of *potential* students with learning difficulties and/or disabilities;

- finally, chapter 6 briefly summarises some information from the study about colleges' overall approaches and strategies towards provision for students with learning difficulties and/or disabilities;

- the report concludes with appendices containing, respectively: detailed tables of statistical findings for the study; the questionnaire used in the survey; a summary of results from research conducted by FEFC statisticians on the incidence of learning difficulties and/or disabilities in the population as a whole and a summary of findings from the parallel survey of external institutions.

13

Mapping Provision: The Provision of and Participation in Further Education by Students with Learning Difficulties and/or Disabilities

ENDNOTES

1 If necessary, using the data from colleges with fuller information to make inferences about the size of this group in the college population as a whole.

2 These were randomly chosen from those external institutions in receipt of funding under the FEFC's additional support bands. Due to the small sample size, the data from external institutions cannot be seen as statistically representative, and rather than incorporating them in the main body of the report, they have been summarised in appendix 4.

3 There were several reasons for this. Firstly, it was clear that a number of colleges, having noted the 1 January completion date, had delayed completion of the survey until after the end of the autumn term, only to discover that the data collection required for the survey was more extensive than they had anticipated, and by this time they had insufficient time to complete the survey by the due date. Secondly, many colleges were unable to complete the survey until the ISR was completed, and it was clear that far fewer colleges than was originally anticipated had submitted their ISR returns by early January 1996. In a number of colleges, pressures of other work and data provision, compounded by problems with management information systems (many colleges were reviewing or updating their MIS) meant that it was not possible to meet the specified deadline.

4 However, with the exception of some key results on overall participation rates, this re-weighting exercise *has not* been undertaken for the present report, since it was judged that there would be little value in attempting this on the basis of incomplete and out-of-date college size data from 1994. Rather, this exercise will be undertaken as and when full data from the November 1995 ISR become available.

Mapping Provision: The Provision of and Participation in Further Education by Students with Learning Difficulties and/or Disabilities

Students with Learning Difficulties and/or Disabilities

Colleges were asked a range of questions about the numbers and characteristics of enrolled students identified as having a learning difficulty and/or disability, as well as about the way in which the institution in question identifies such students.

Numbers of students with learning difficulties and/or disabilities

20   Colleges responding to the survey were asked to indicate how many students enrolled at the institution (as at 1 November 1995) had been identified as having a learning difficulty and/or disability (irrespective of whether they had been identified as needing any learning support or additional support).

21   Among the responding colleges, 272 of the 274 were able to provide full data on the total number of students identified as having learning difficulties and/or disabilities. Summed across the 272 colleges, 81,892 students with learning difficulties and/or disabilities were recorded, an average of just

over 300 for each institution[1]. The number of such students in an individual institution varied from zero to 2,735. Table 4 shows the distribution of respondent institutions by broad grouping of numbers of students with learning difficulties and/or disabilities.

22   Of particular interest, however, is to ascertain not just how many enrolled students with learning difficulties and/or disabilities there are, but what proportion of total enrolments they account for, and how this share varies between colleges of different types and sizes, and according to other student characteristics.

23   Unfortunately, the extent to which these issues can be analysed at this stage is limited by the fact that the only data available to us on overall college enrolments refer, in most cases, to the corresponding point in the previous year (November 1994). On the assumption that total college populations have not changed dramatically over the year in question, expressing the current student population with learning difficulties and/or

Table 4.   Colleges responding by numbers of students with learning difficulties and/or disabilities

Students with learning difficulties and/or disabilities	Colleges responding	
	No.	%
0–99	85	31.3
100–299	92	33.8
300 or more	95	34.9
Total (N=100%)	272	100.0

disabilities as a share of total student population in 1994 should still enable some examination of broad patterns of participation. As the full 1995 ISR data become available, it will be a straightforward exercise to update the estimates presented here. However, all results presented in this report which include data based on total college populations (including all breakdowns by college size, and all estimates of the share of students with learning difficulties and/or disabilities) should be treated as *provisional,* and subject to amendment on the basis of 1995 ISR data.

24   Taking the 272 responding colleges for which the relevant data were available, the total number of enrolled students (November 1994) was 1,439,923, and the total number of students (November 1995) with learning difficulties and/or disabilities was 81,892, that is, students with learning difficulties and/or disabilities accounted for an estimated 5.7% of the enrolled student population[2].

25   Looking at the same data from the perspective of the individual college, the average share (for each college) of enrolled students with learning difficulties and/or

disabilities was 6.4%, but the median share was 4.3% (that is, the overall average is again boosted by a small number of colleges with large percentages of students with learning difficulties and/or disabilities).

26   A key question is, how does the share of students with learning difficulties and/or disabilities vary between college types? Figure 1[3] shows, for colleges of each of the six types, the share of enrolled students with learning difficulties and/or disabilities across colleges of the type in question. The most notable feature of the table is the lack of significant variation by college type in this share — at least as far as the most numerous college types are concerned. Thus, with the exception of agriculture and horticulture colleges (18 in total), which stand out as having a higher-than-average share of students with learning difficulties and/or disabilities (8.2%), and the specialist designated institutions (seven in total), which have a much lower than average share (1.4%), the other college types all have shares very close to the overall population average (between 5.4% and 5.8%).

27   Repeating the same analysis by region, however, the data reveal rather greater

Figure 1.   Share of students with learning difficulties and/or disabilities by type of institution

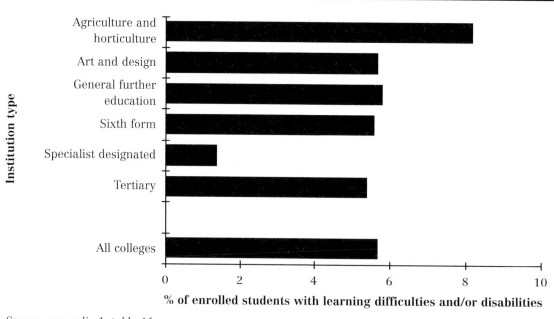

Source: appendix 1, table A1

variation in the share of enrolled students with learning difficulties and/or disabilities (figure 2) from a low of 3.4% in Greater London to a high of 7.8% in the West Midlands. It should be noted, however, that the estimates are based on small numbers of cases in some of the regions and some caution should, therefore, be exercised in interpreting these results at a regional level.

28   Furthermore, it is possible that regional variations reflect differences in the composition of colleges by region, and that certain regions contain higher proportions of college types associated with higher shares of students with learning difficulties and/or disabilities. One possible dimension of variation here is college size and figure 3 shows how the share of enrolled students with learning difficulties and/or disabilities varies with the overall number of enrolled students in the college. The figure confirms that the share of such students tends to vary with college size — specifically, the smallest colleges would appear to have the largest share of students with learning disabilities and/or disabilities, and the share tends to decrease with college size. The pattern is slightly more complex than revealed by the

figure, however, since a further breakdown of the data shows that the share of such students begins to increase again in the largest colleges (the share falls to 3.8% among colleges with between 7,500 and 9,999 students, but rises again to 6.4% among those with 10,000 or more students).

29   Although it is clear from the above that the share of students with learning difficulties and/or disabilities varies both between regions, and with college size, it does not appear that the regional variation is primarily due to the fact that different regions contain different size distributions of colleges. Figure 4 shows how the average size of colleges varies between region. The overall national average is 5,300, but the regional averages vary from a low of 4,000 in the East Midlands to a high of 7,200 in the North West. This variation in average college size does not appear to be correlated with the regional variation in college shares of students with learning difficulties and/or disabilities recorded in figure 2, however. Thus, for example, although we know that larger colleges have a lower share of students with learning disabilities and/or disabilities, the regions with the largest average college size

Figure 2.   Share of students with learning difficulties and/or disabilities by FEFC region

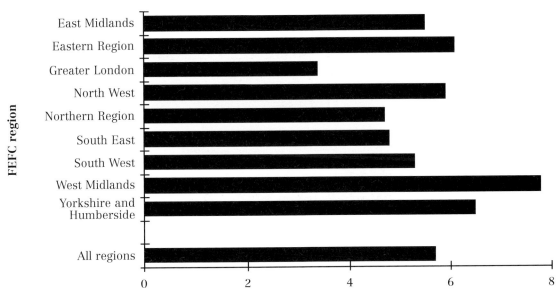

% of enrolled students with learning difficulties and/or disabilities

Source: appendix 1, table A2

do not appear to be the regions with the lowest shares of these students.

30   There appears to be both a 'size effect' and a 'regional effect', and the regions which seem to be achieving higher participation rates are not doing so simply as a result of the size or structure of the colleges in the regions in question. It is, however, possible that the different *balance* of college types between regions may have made a difference here. It is, for example, notable that nearly all of the specialist designated institutions (with low shares of students with learning difficulties and/or disabilities) are located in the Greater London region, and this fact has tended to lower the average share of students with learning difficulties and/or disabilities in this region.

Figure 3.   Share of students with learning difficulties and/or disabilities by college size

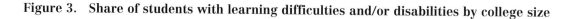
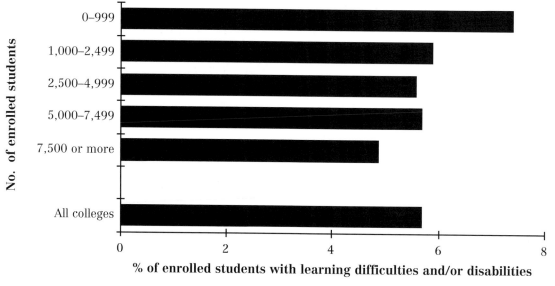

Source: appendix 1, table A3
Note: college size as at November 1994

Figure 4.   Variation in size of surveyed colleges by FEFC region

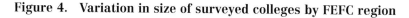
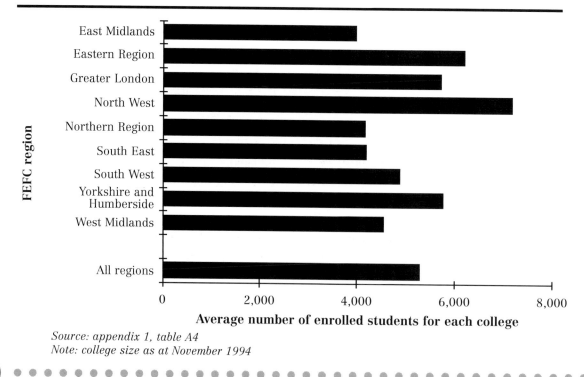

Source: appendix 1, table A4
Note: college size as at November 1994

Mapping Provision: The Provision of and Participation in Further Education by Students with Learning Difficulties and/or Disabilities

31   A further key question, however, given this variation in participation by college size, and given also the variation in survey response rates by size noted above, is how our overall estimate of a 5.7% share of enrolled students with learning difficulties and/or disabilities is affected when we weight the survey data to make them representative of the college population by institution size. In practice, despite the significant variation by size category, the re-weighting exercise does not affect the overall estimate significantly[4]. Thus, applying the estimated shares of students with learning difficulties and/or disabilities in each of the six size categories to the total student population estimates for those categories (derived from the November 1994 ISR) yields a grossed-up total for England as a whole of 126,542 students with learning difficulties and/or disabilities (that is, again some 5.7% of the enrolled student population in November 1994[5]).

32   It must be recognised, however, that in so far as overall enrolments increased between November 1994 and November 1995 (the latter being the date to which the survey refers) this figure of 5.7% is likely to be an *over-estimate* of the participation rate. How much of an over-estimate is likely to be difficult to assess at this stage. At the time of writing, however, there are data available indicating the growth in enrolled student numbers for 299 sector colleges. If we apply the rates of growth (over 1994-95) in student enrolments recorded in these colleges to the November 1994 enrolments data for November 1995 (using separate growth rates for full-time and part-time students; and for colleges of each of the six main types), we find that November enrolments in the sector as a whole grew by some 7.1% over the year (from 2.23 to 2.39 million). If we assume also that no other relevant changes in enrolment patterns occurred over the period[6], this would imply that our estimate of 126,500 students with learning difficulties and/or disabilities represented some 5.3% of the overall enrolled student population at November 1995.

Student characteristics

33   Respondents were asked further to break down the data on their enrolled students with learning difficulties and/or disabilities according to sex, mode of attendance (full-time or part-time), age, and ethnicity. Table 5 summarises the data provided. The table also gives, for comparative purposes, estimates of the same breakdown for the enrolled student population as a whole[7].

Sex

34   Looking first at sex, the relevant data were provided by 252 out of the 274 colleges, and of the 73,400 students with learning difficulties and/or disabilities enrolled in these colleges 49.2% were female. This suggests that female students with learning difficulties and/or disabilities are under-represented compared with the representation of female students (54.6%) in the overall enrolled student population. There was some variation in the breakdown across different types of colleges, with the share of students with learning difficulties and/or disabilities who were female varying from a low of under 40% in art and design colleges to a high of 55% in specialist designated institutions (see table A8 in appendix 1). This variation was, however, almost entirely due to the share of part-time students with learning difficulties and/or disabilities (part-time students were more likely to be female, and full-time students to be male — see paragraph 35). There was a similar variation by college size (table A10 in appendix 1), with larger colleges having a higher share of female students with learning difficulties and/or disabilities, but again this was strongly linked to the share of part-time students (smaller colleges, particularly sixth form colleges, having much lower shares of part-timers than their larger counterparts). There was no notable regional variation (see table A9 in appendix 1).

19

Mode of attendance

35   Turning then to the full-time/part-time split itself (also shown in table 5), 262 out of the 274 colleges gave such information, and of the 79,074 students with learning difficulties and/or disabilities in these colleges, 45% were full-timers, and the rest were part-time students. The representation of part-timers among students with learning difficulties and/or disabilities is lower than the share of part-time students in the overall enrolled student population. What is not clear, however, is the extent to which this difference may reflect an identification issue — thus, if some colleges adopt a less extensive identification/assessment process for part-time students (as suggested by table 7 on page 24), it is likely that some part-time students with less apparent learning difficulties and/or disabilities will be less likely to be recorded as such than their full-time counterparts.

36   There is a link between the relative under-representation among students with learning difficulties and/or disabilities of female students on the one hand, and of part-time students on the other. The survey data confirmed that female students with learning difficulties and/or disabilities were slightly more likely to be part time than their male counterparts. For the 252 colleges providing full information on both sex and attendance mode, 51.1% of part-time students were female, as against 47% of full-timers.

37   The incidence of part-time students with learning difficulties and/or disabilities varied dramatically between colleges of different types (see table A5 in appendix 1), with sixth form colleges having very few (14%), compared with general further education colleges (58%), and at the extreme, specialist designated institutions with 86%. There was also some size variation (see table A7 in appendix 1) with the part-time share being greater in the largest colleges than in the smallest colleges (reflecting, at least in part, the over-representation of sixth form, and art and design colleges among the smallest

institutions, and general further education colleges among the largest). These variations by size and college type were generally similar to the pattern of variation in the share of part-time students within the overall enrolled student population (shown in table 5), although in every college type, and in every size group, the share of students with learning difficulties and/or disabilities who were part-time, was lower than the share of part-timers among the corresponding overall student population.

38   Regional variations in part-time incidence were also evident (see table A6 in appendix 1) with, at one end of the scale, 40% of students with learning difficulties and/or disabilities being part time in the South East, compared with a figure of nearly 65% in Yorkshire and Humberside at the other end of the scale. Again, however, these differences also reflect the part-time/full-time split in the overall student populations in the different regions which, in turn, are partly influenced by the balance of college types in different regions — the South East, for example, has the largest concentration of sixth form colleges.

Age

39   Information on students' age (table 5) was provided by 249 colleges, and of the 64,049 students with learning difficulties and/or disabilities enrolled in these institutions, 50.8% were 25 years old or older, 32.8% were 16 to 18 year olds, and 16.4% were 19 to 24 year olds. This age distribution corresponded very closely to that for the enrolled student population as a whole.

40   As might be expected, there was a strong correlation between age and mode of attendance among students with learning difficulties and/or disabilities. Thus, among 16 to 18 year olds, 19.8% of students with learning difficulties and/or disabilities are part time, among 19 to 24 year olds the proportion of part-timers rises to 50.6%, whilst among students aged 25 and over it is still higher at 78.7%.

20

Mapping Provision: The Provision of and Participation in Further Education by Students with Learning Difficulties and/or Disabilities

Table 5.   Characteristics of students with learning difficulties and/or disabilities

Characteristic	Students	Colleges on which estimate is based	Estimates for the overall student population
	%	No.	
Sex	252		
Males	50.8		45.4
Females	49.2		54.6
Mode of attendance		262	
Full-time students	45.0		34.8
Part-time students	55.0		65.2
Age		249	
Under 16 year olds			1.5
16–18 year olds	32.8		31.3
19–24 year olds	16.4		17.9
25 and older	50.8		49.2
Ethnic origin		248	
White	79.8		72.8
Black-Caribbean	1.7		1.9
Black-African	0.6		1.3
Black-other	0.5		0.6
Indian	1.6		2.1
Pakistani	2.3		1.9
Bangladeshi	0.3		0.9
Chinese	0.4		0.5
Other Asian	0.5		0.4
Other	1.2		1.8
Ethnic group unknown	10.9		15.9
All students	**100.0**	**232**	**100.0**

Note: college size as at November 1994; 348 colleges

41   Unsurprisingly, therefore, the age distributions of the student population with learning difficulties and/or disabilities, by institution type, region and college size (tables A8, A9 and A10 respectively in appendix 1) broadly correspond to the part-time/full-time splits discussed above. In crude terms, smaller colleges (among which sixth form, and art and design colleges are over-represented) tend to have younger populations of students with learning difficulties and/or disabilities, whilst larger institutions (among which general further education colleges are over-represented) have much larger representations of adult students with learning difficulties and/or disabilities. The regional pattern also reinforces the pattern observed in terms of mode of attendance (see paragraphs 35 to 38), with the South East standing out as having a younger-than-average student population with learning difficulties and/or disabilities, whilst the North West and Yorkshire and Humberside lie at the other end of the scale with high proportions of such students aged 25 and over.

Ethnicity

42   Of the 274 colleges, 248 provided data on ethnicity, accounting between them for 73,660 enrolled students with learning difficulties and/or disabilities. The ethnic origin of a significant minority of these students (nearly 11%) was unknown, but of those whose ethnic origin was identified, some 10.3% were non-white (table 5 shows the detailed ethnic categories — the largest non-white group is Pakistanis, followed by Black Caribbeans and Indians respectively). The data on ethnicity are hard to compare with those for the enrolled student population as a whole, and the small size of most of the ethnic minority groups mean that statistical margins of error are relatively large. What does seem clear, however, is that compared with the overall student population, white students with learning difficulties are somewhat over-represented, and non-white students correspondingly under-represented.

43   Table A11 (in appendix 1) shows considerable variation by college type in the ethnic composition of the student population with learning difficulties and/or disabilities, with agriculture and horticulture colleges, and art and design colleges standing out as having very small shares of non-white students. The very large share of students with learning difficulties and/or disabilities recorded as being non-white in specialist designated institutions reflects at least in part the fact that some of these colleges appear to have included ESOL students in their returns[8].

44   Regional patterns (see table A12 in appendix 1) in part mirrored the uneven distribution of the ethnic minority population across the country, with high shares of non-white students with learning difficulties and/or disabilities in the East Midlands and West Midlands regions, Yorkshire and Humberside and Greater London[9], and correspondingly low shares in the Northern Region and the North West and South East regions.

Type and level of learning programme being followed

'Inclusive' vs 'discrete' provision

45   Table 6 summarises responses to a question which attempted to identify the extent to which 'inclusive' or 'integrated' approaches to provision for students with learning difficulties and/or disabilities had been adopted by colleges (as opposed to 'discrete' provision[10]).

Table 6.   Type of learning programme being followed

Programme type		Students with learning difficulties and/or disabilities following programmes of type				Part-time students
		Full-time	Part-time	All students		
		No.	No.	No.	%	%
a)	Programme designed for any student	20,593	17,890	38,483	52.8	46.5
b)	Programme designed solely or primarily for students with learning difficulties and/or disabilities	8,825	22,455	31,280	42.9	71.8
c)	Programme combining elements of a) and b) above	1,951	1,219	3,170	4.3	38.5
Total (N=100%)		**31,369**	**41,564**	**72,933**	**100.0**	**57.0**

Note: based on 254 colleges

46 Table 6 shows that similar numbers of students are following programmes of the two broad types, with just over 50% of students with learning difficulties and/or disabilities following 'inclusive/integrated' type programmes, and just under 50% following programmes of the 'discrete' type, or which include 'discrete' components. A much higher share of students on 'discrete' programmes are part-timers, than for the other programme types.

47 Table A14 (in appendix 1) breaks down these responses by type of institution, and shows considerable variation between the different college types. At one end of the scale, sixth form colleges, and art and design colleges, report that most of their students with learning difficulties and/or disabilities follow 'programmes designed for any student', whilst at the other end of the scale 75% of students with learning difficulties and/or disabilities in specialist designated institutions are following 'discrete' programmes[11]. Tertiary and general further education colleges are close to the average, with around 50% of their students on 'inclusive' provision.

48 Regional and college size variations in the type of learning programme being followed by students with learning difficulties and/or disabilities (see tables A15 and A16 in appendix 1) largely reflected the balance of college types. Thus, the share of students receiving 'discrete' provision increased with college size, whilst regions with low shares of discrete provision tended to be regions (such as the South East and North West) with relatively large numbers of sixth form colleges.

Level of learning programme followed

49 Similarly, figure 5 shows the percentage of students with learning difficulties and/or disabilities following programmes of different levels (broadly defined). Figure 5 makes clear the concentration of these students in lower-level programmes, with nearly 50% of them following pre-vocational or foundation level programmes, and only 16% following

programmes at (G)NVQ level 3 or above (or equivalent). This contrasts with an estimated 41% of all students enrolled at further education colleges following programmes at level 3 or above[12].

50 As might be expected, however, the pattern varies considerably between college types, as table A18 (in appendix 1) confirms. Thus, art and design colleges, and sixth form colleges have much lower than average shares of students with learning difficulties and/or disabilities following pre-vocational/ foundation courses (5% and 16% respectively), and much higher than average proportions following courses at (G)NVQ level 3 or above (79% and 54% respectively). These differences between college type are then reflected in regional and college size differences, with smaller colleges, and regions with larger numbers of sixth form colleges recording more students on higher level learning programmes than the average (see tables A19 and A20 in appendix 1).

Identification of learning difficulties and/or disabilities

51 Colleges were asked how (if at all) they attempted formally to identify enrolled students who have a learning difficulty and/or disability, and also whether these methods differed between full-time and part-time students. The responses are summarised in table 7.

52 Table 7 shows that the vast majority of colleges (over 90%) attempted to identify students with learning difficulties and/or disabilities irrespective of whether they need learning support (although in about 33% of these colleges this blanket approach applied only to full-time students). A small minority of colleges (particularly for part-time students) relied on self-identification of learning difficulties and/or disabilities, and/or only tried to identify such students where there was a learning support need.

53 Further breakdowns of the data showed that the approach to identification of learning difficulties and/or disabilities varied

significantly according to college type, and to the size of the enrolled student population with learning difficulties and/or disabilities. Thus, table 8 shows the proportions of institutions of different types which claim to identify all students (either full-time only or both full-time and part-time) with learning difficulties and/or disabilities irrespective of any learning support need. The most notable variation is between sixth form colleges (and to a lesser extent art and design colleges), and other types of college (the former being much more likely to take such an approach only for full-time students).

54   It should be borne in mind that where comparisons between college types are made, important differences in size and function exist

Figure 5.   Level of learning programme being followed by students with learning difficulties and/or disabilities

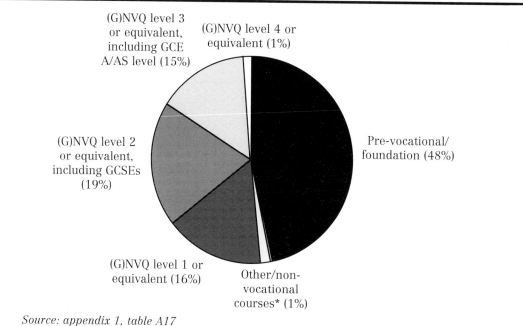

(G)NVQ level 3 or equivalent, including GCE A/AS level (15%)

(G)NVQ level 4 or equivalent (1%)

(G)NVQ level 2 or equivalent, including GCSEs (19%)

Pre-vocational/ foundation (48%)

(G)NVQ level 1 or equivalent (16%)

Other/non-vocational courses* (1%)

Source: appendix 1, table A17
*see note to table A17, appendix 1

Table 7.   Identification of students with learning difficulties and/or disabilities

Identification method	Colleges (N = 271) using method for		
	full-time students	*part-time students*	*full-time and part-time students*
	%	%	%
Institution attempts to identify all students with learning difficulties and/or disabilities irrespective of whether they need learning support	29.2	0.0	62.7
Students with learning difficulties and/or disabilities are identified only through self-identification	0.0	9.2	5.5
Students with learning difficulties and/or disabilities are identified only where there is a learning support need	0.0	7.0	6.6

Note: columns and rows do not sum to 100% as some institutions fell into more than one category

between college types. In particular, it should be noted that sixth form colleges are much smaller on average than tertiary and general further education colleges and remain (despite recent diversification in provision) much more heavily focused on full-time GCE A level provision than is the case for other college types.

55   Table 9 shows that the more students with learning difficulties and/or disabilities an institution has, the more likely it is to identify all students with learning difficulties and/or disabilities irrespective of learning support need (the colleges with small

numbers of such students are more likely to have such an approach only for their full-time students). This pattern may partly also reflect the possibility that colleges with comprehensive identification strategies are more likely to identify and record their enrolled students with learning difficulties and/or disabilities and, therefore, to show up in the data as having larger numbers of such students.

56   Table 10 extends this analysis, and shows that the overall size of the college is important as well — in general terms, the

Table 8.   Identification approach by type of institution

Institution type		Respondents identifying all students with learning difficulties and/or disabilities irrespective of learning support needs	
		Full-time students	Full-time & part-time students
	No.	%	%
Agriculture and horticulture college	18	33.3	66.7
Art and design college	7	42.9	57.1
General further education college	137	13.9	75.9
Sixth form college	66	60.6	36.4
Specialist designated institution	7	57.1	0.0
Tertiary college	36	19.4	72.2
Total (N = 100%)	271	29.2	62.7

Table 9.   Identification approach by number of students with learning difficulties and/or disabilities

Number of students with learning difficulties and/or disabilities in institution		Respondents identifying all students with learning difficulties and/or disabilities irrespective of learning support needs	
		Full-time students	Full-time & part-time students
	No.	%	%
0–99	85	52.9	41.2
100–299	92	20.7	71.7
300 or more	92	16.3	73.9
Total (=100%)	269	29.2	62.7

25

larger a college is, the more likely it is to identify all students (both full-time and part-time) with learning difficulties and/or disabilities irrespective of learning support need (once again, this is likely to reflect the over-representation of sixth form colleges, in particular, among the smallest colleges).

57   To conclude the analysis of colleges' approaches towards identification and assessment, respondents were asked whether there were students enrolled in their institution who have a learning difficulty and/or disability, but who have not been formally identified as such. Where respondents said 'yes' to this question, they were further asked whether it was possible to make a broad estimate of the number of such students. Those answering 'yes' again were asked for the number in question (distinguishing, if possible between full-time and part-time students). Responses are summarised in table 11.

58   Clearly, given that this question relates to students presumed or known to have learning difficulties and/or disabilities, but who have not been formally identified as such, the information presented in table 11

must be seen as indicative only. Of particular interest, however, is the fact that a significant proportion of colleges (44%) believe that they have students with learning difficulties and/or disabilities not formally identified, and a further 21% do not know (but accept that they may have such students). Of those who believe this, however, 38% (or 17% of all respondents) can make a broad estimate of how many such students they might have. In total, such estimates (made by 46 colleges) amount to over 5,400, an average of 118 for each college (although the total is skewed significantly by one college estimating that it has some 3,000 students in this category — excluding this college reduces the average to 54 students for each college).

59   Finally, only 40 colleges made an estimated breakdown of these students between full-timers and part-timers, but (contrary to our expectations) this does not suggest that part-time students with a learning difficulty and/or disability are less likely than their full-time counterparts to have their learning difficulty and/or disability formally identified; if anything the reverse is true.

Table 10.   Identification approach by size of college

Enrolled students	*Respondents identifying all students with learning difficulties and/or disabilities irrespective of learning support needs*		
		Full-time students	*Full-time & part-time students*
	No.	*%*	*%*
0–999	43	51.2	44.2
1,000–2,499	57	54.4	40.4
2,500–4,999	44	25.0	61.4
5,000–7,499	60	11.7	83.3
7,500–9,999	28	10.7	82.1
10,000 or more	39	12.8	71.8
Total (N = 100%)	**271**	**29.2**	**62.7**

Note: college size as at November 1994

Table 11. Estimated numbers of students with learning difficulties and/or disabilities not formally identified

	Yes		No		Don't know		No answer		N =
	N°	%	N°	%	N°	%	N°	%	
College responding to 'Are there students enrolled in the institution who have a learning difficulty and/or disability but who have not been formally identified as such?'	121	44.2	93	33.9	57	20.8	3	1.1	274
'Is it possible to make a broad estimate of the number of such students?'	46	38.0	61	50.4	14	11.6			121
Estimate of total number of such students (summed across colleges making estimate)	5,431*								46

		Full-time	Part-time	40
of which		1,110	799	

* includes one institution with 3,000 estimated students

ENDNOTES

1 The mean (or average) number of students with learning difficulties and/or disabilities in each college was 301, and the median value was 204 (the median is the value which divides the distribution in half, that is, the number of students in the college compared with which, half the colleges had a larger number, and half had a smaller number of students with learning difficulties and/or disabilities). This difference between the mean and the median is because the mean value is boosted by the influence of a small number of colleges with very large numbers of such students.

2 Note that, as explained in appendix 3, a key conclusion from part A of the study is that it is not currently possible to make statistically reliable comparisons between estimates of the share of enrolled students in further education who have learning difficulties and/or disabilities on the one hand, and external estimates of the incidence of learning difficulties/disabilities in the overall population on the other hand.

3 Note that, throughout the rest of the report, where information is presented in the form of a figure or chart, the corresponding data are to be found in a table in appendix 1.

4 This is largely because the effect of a general decline in the share of students with learning difficulties and/or disabilities as college size increases is offset by the increase in the share among the very largest colleges. It should be stressed that this is true on the basis of the 1994 ISR-based weights used here. As already noted, however, this exercise needs to be repeated as and when full up-to-date college enrolment estimates based on the November 1995 ISR become available.

5 In addition, it should be noted that there is a small number (1,755 in March 1996) of students with learning difficulties and/or disabilities (typically more severe than the average) for whom provision, funded by the FEFC, is made outside the sector (mainly in specialist establishments, not covered in the present study).

6 For example, in the distribution of enrolments between colleges of different sizes, remember that our overall participation estimates are based on grossing up on the basis of college size, rather than institution type.

7 Once again these figures are based on information provided to us by the FEFC, derived from returns (348 colleges in total) from the November 1994 ISR, which allow us to make broad comparisons with our own survey information from November 1995.

8 Where possible we have removed such students from the data if they did not also have a learning difficulty and/or disability. In some colleges, however, the recording systems used did not permit this.

9 Note, however, that the very high share recorded in Greater London largely reflects the fact that six out of the seven specialist designated institutions in the study are located in this region and, as already discussed, there are reasons to believe that the ethnicity data from these colleges may be inconsistent due to the inclusion of ESOL students in some cases.

10 Note that a small minority of colleges did not provide this information and, as a result, the total number of students referred to in table 6 is slightly less than the overall total (being based on data from some 254 colleges).

11 Again, a significant proportion of these may be ESOL courses.

12 Source: FEFC Press Release, 30 April 1996; data grossed up from 327 colleges submitting November 1995 ISR returns.

Nature of Learning Difficulties and/or Disabilities and Learning Support Received

Incidence of type of learning difficulty

60 Table 12 summarises the information requested from respondents on the incidence of specific types of learning difficulty and/or disability among their enrolled student population.

61 Although this question was generally well-answered by respondents there were, nevertheless, a number of difficulties experienced by colleges in providing the information in question[1]. In many cases colleges' own information systems did not record the nature of the learning difficulty and/or disability in question, and even where this was recorded, a number of different classification systems were in use. Partly as a result of these difficulties, exacerbated in a small number of cases by inappropriate completion of the questionnaire (for example, some respondents, contrary to the survey instructions, included people with ESOL or basic skills needs, but who did not otherwise have a learning difficulty and/or disability[2]), the total number of students included in table 12 differs somewhat from the total number of students with learning difficulties and/or disabilities identified above (see paragraphs 20 to 25). Considerable effort has been devoted to reducing some of these internal inconsistencies in the data (in some cases through extensive further contact with the college(s) in question), but it should be

recognised, in the light of the difficulties in collating the data, that table 12 provides only a very broad picture of the distribution of enrolled students by type of learning difficulty and/or disability. Table 12 also shows the proportion of students with learning difficulties and/or disabilities of each type who are receiving learning support, and the proportion of the latter whose learning support is FEFC-funded (wholly or in part).

62 Overall, table 12 shows that nearly 60% of students with a learning difficulty and/or disability are identified as receiving learning support, and just over 70% of these students receive learning support which is wholly or partly funded by the FEFC's additional support bands. Putting the two items together suggests that 45% of students with learning difficulties and/or disabilities receive learning support which is wholly or partly FEFC funded.

63 Tables A21 and A22 in appendix 1 show how the incidence of different types of learning difficulty and/or disability among enrolled students varies by institution type and college size. There are a few differences between institution types in this respect. Particularly notable is the very high share of students with learning difficulties and/or disabilities in sixth form, and art and design colleges who are recorded as having specific learning difficulties (such as dyslexia).

29

Mapping Provision: The Provision of and Participation in Further Education by Students with Learning Difficulties and/or Disabilities

Table 12. Incidence of different types of learning difficulty and/or disability among enrolled students, and learning support received

Characteristics of learning difficulty and/or disability	Enrolled students		Receiving learning support*	Receiving support funded through FEFC additional support bands*
	No.	%	%	%
Moderate learning difficulties	14,257	18.9	88.0	75.4
Severe learning difficulties	11,402	15.1	85.6	81.6
Unspecified/unknown	10,578	14.0	9.0	38.3
Specific learning difficulties (for example, dyslexia, dyscalcula)	6,787	9.0	76.6	75.3
Other medical conditions (for example, epilepsy, asthma, diabetes)	6,162	8.2	20.7	46.9
Multiple disabilities	4,757	6.3	80.8	79.4
Mental ill health	3,334	4.4	77.5	64.3
Hearing impairment	3,282	4.4	55.3	72.3
Disability affecting mobility	3,253	4.3	51.1	64.4
Basic skills/ESOL needs[+]	3,141	4.2	54.6	54.6
Visual impairment	2,678	3.5	51.0	60.8
Other physical disability	2,232	3.0	50.3	50.5
Emotional/behavioural difficulties	1,269	1.7	82.1	72.6
Other[‡]	1,159	1.5	62.3	78.8
Profound/complex disabilities	829	1.1	95.3	60.3
Temporary disability after illness (for example, post-viral) or accident	321	0.4	59.1	66.5
Total	**75,441**	**100.0**	**63.2**	**71.4**

there were a number of respondents reporting the number of enrolled students in a given disability category, but who did not also indicate whether those students were receiving learning support and/or the source of funding of that support. The percentages indicated in this column, therefore, are calculated after these respondents have been excluded from the total, and the estimates in these columns are, as a result, generally based on smaller numbers of respondents than are the enrolled student estimates in the first column

[+] *'basic skills/ESOL needs' should not have been included in responses to this question. Some respondents did, however, despite the questionnaire instructions, include them and they are listed here*

[‡] *the 'other' category included a range of disabilities and conditions identified by respondents, including: cystic fibrosis; cerebral palsy; specific academic difficulty; semantic pragmatic disorder; Down's syndrome; spina bifida; Asperger's syndrome; Tourette's syndrome; mild learning difficulties; RSI; anorexia; Ménière's disease; depression; heart transplants and some others. As far as possible these have been re-categorised into one of the general categories identified in the questionnaire, and this residual category includes those that could not be so re-categorised*

64   Equally marked is the very low incidence of moderate, and especially severe learning difficulties in sixth form colleges. Many of the other variations, however, involve small numbers of students and are unlikely to be significant, although some patterns are consistent with our expectations (thus, for example, the incidence of students with visual impairments is similar across most groups of colleges, but is much lower than average among students in art and design colleges, and in agriculture and horticulture colleges). Differences according to college size are also quite marked, and consistent with those observed between college types. Thus, for example, larger colleges tend to have a higher share of students with severe learning difficulties, students with multiple or profound disabilities, and students with mental illness, and a lower share of students with specific learning difficulties.

Table 13. Nature of learning support provision offered

Nature of facility/support provision	(a) Colleges with students receiving support/provision in question		(b) Colleges in (a) where support is wholly or partly funded through FEFC additional support bands
	No.	%	%
Support assistants (non-teaching)	215	78.5	90.7
Supplementary teaching (outside main course)	198	72.3	85.4
Specialist equipment	185	67.5	32.4
Specialist assessment	185	67.5	71.4
Communicators/specialist teaching (for hearing impaired students)	180	65.7	85.0
Drop-in support centres (for example, basic skills workshops)	171	62.4	62.6
Specialist careers advice	157	57.3	20.4
Educational psychology	153	55.8	71.2
Transport between home and the institution	150	54.7	11.3
Class support from additional teacher	148	54.0	83.1
Cross-institution learning support team(s)	144	52.6	72.9
Specialist teaching for blind/partially-sighted students	120	43.8	80.0
Social work support	111	40.5	9.9
Transport between sites	107	39.1	60.7
Taping/brailling	98	35.8	75.5
Speech/communication/language therapy	75	27.4	37.3
Specialist counselling for disabled people	62	22.6	61.3
Nursing support/medical services	55	20.1	23.6
Specialist psychiatric support	55	20.1	29.1
Physiotherapy	43	15.7	16.3
Total (N=100%)	**274**	**100.0**	

Note: figures sum to more than 100% as respondents were able to indicate several categories of support

65   Table 13 shows the number of colleges offering learning support and support facilities of different types to students with learning difficulties and/or disabilities.

66   The corresponding information, broken down by institution type and college size can be found in tables A23 and A24 (in appendix 1). The most notable finding from these tables is that virtually all types of learning support provision were more widespread in general further education colleges and tertiary colleges than in sixth form colleges, art and design, or agriculture and horticulture colleges. Similarly, and not surprisingly, there was a strong general tendency for the incidence of most types of

learning support provision to increase with college size (although the very largest colleges did not always have a greater range of provision than those in the second size band). Beyond this, it is difficult to summarise the patterns reported and the reader is, therefore, referred to the detailed tables for information on the extent to which different types of support provision were offered by different types of college.

67   The questionnaire also asked respondents, where possible, to indicate the number of students in receipt of each type of learning support, but not all were able to provide such information. Table 13 is confined, therefore, to indicating whether or

Table 14. Students receiving learning support

Nature of facility/support provision	Students in each college receiving support or using facility Average no.	Colleges providing data No.
Support assistants (non-teaching)	53.8	227
Cross-institution learning support team(s)	48.4	210
Drop-in support centres (for example, basic skills workshops)	48.3	201
Class support from additional teacher	33.7	232
Specialist assessment	30.6	209
Supplementary teaching (outside main course)	27.8	223
Specialist careers advice	28.7	219
Transport between home and the institution	12.7	238
Social work support	10.4	235
Educational psychology	8.9	224
Specialist equipment	8.3	230
Transport between sites	9.1	235
Communicators/specialist teaching (for hearing impaired students)	5.1	246
Specialist psychiatric support	4.4	256
Specialist counselling for disabled people	4.2	247
Nursing support/medical services	2.5	250
Specialist teaching for blind/partially-sighted students	2.4	255
Speech/communication/language therapy	1.8	254
Taping/brailling	1.6	252
Physiotherapy	1.0	261

not the college offered such support, and if so whether or not the support was (wholly or partly) funded through the FEFC additional support bands.

68   In table 14, however, we provide information from a smaller subset of colleges on the numbers of students covered by each type of learning support. It is not possible to calculate the percentage of students in receipt of each type of learning support, since a number of respondents were able to indicate the numbers in receipt of some kinds of support, but for other kinds of support were able only to indicate that the support was offered (and not the numbers of students receiving it). Table 14 must, given the variable numbers of respondents in each row, be interpreted with some caution therefore, and because of this variation, we have presented the information in terms of the average number of students for each college in receipt of the support in question.

69   As might be expected, the ranking of different types of support according to the numbers of students receiving them differs somewhat from their ranking in terms of the numbers of colleges offering them. The support types affecting the largest average numbers of students (table 14) tend to be those which are not specific to particular types of student or disability and/or learning difficulty — such as cross-institution learning support teams, or drop-in centres. By contrast, there are some facilities offered by relatively large numbers of colleges (table 13), but which are provided to relatively small average numbers of students (table 14) — communicators/specialist teaching for hearing-impaired students are of this nature, for example.

70   Finally, in this context, respondents were also asked to indicate (although this was not the primary focus of the survey) how many students were in receipt of additional support funding from FEFC for reasons *other* than a learning difficulty and/or disability — for example, students with basic skills needs

(literacy and/or numeracy) not related to a learning difficulty and/or disability; and ESOL students[3]. Some 212 colleges provided such data, and the number of students receiving learning support for non-learning difficulty and/or disability-related reasons in these colleges was 22,617 (an average of 107 for each college).

71   The data in table 12 imply that just over 34,000 students were receiving FEFC-funded learning support[4] for reasons associated with learning difficulties and/or disabilities; these latter data, however, refer to a larger number of responding colleges. If we take only those 189 colleges providing data on both categories, that is, students receiving FEFC-funded support for learning difficulty and/or disability-related reasons and those receiving FEFC-funded learning support for other reasons, there are 25,906 students in the first category and 21,486 in the second, implying that overall, in these colleges, some 45.3% of students receiving funding through the FEFC additional support bands are doing so for reasons not associated with a learning difficulty and/or disability in the sense defined here. Clearly some caution needs to be exercised (given the low levels of response to the question) in grossing up from these results to make overall estimates for the whole population. They do suggest, nevertheless, that a significant share (perhaps close to 50%) of students funded through the additional support bands do not have a learning difficulty and/or disability in the sense defined by the committee.

ENDNOTES

1 As noted in earlier stages of the research, in a significant number of institutions, particularly those adopting an 'inclusive' approach to provision in this area, it was felt that even to attempt to categorise students in this fashion was potentially inimical to the underlying philosophy and college strategy on learning support provision.

2 In a number of cases, this was simply a practical issue, and was because record systems did not allow colleges to separate out such students. In others an issue of principle was involved in the sense that a number of colleges argued that a student with a serious literacy and/or numeracy problem, for example, could be seen as having a learning difficulty by definition, and that such a student *should not*, therefore, be excluded from the data.

3 That is, students requiring support because their first language is not English.

4 That is, learning support funded through the FEFC additional support bands.

Cost of and Funding for Learning Support

● ●

FEFC additional support bands

72   Respondents were asked to indicate the numbers of students whose additional support is funded through the FEFC, in each of the FEFC's additional support bands for annual cost for each student (including only those with learning difficulties and/or disabilities, and excluding those with other learning support needs — such as basic skills, ESOL — who do not also have a learning difficulty and/or disability). The responses (from 215 colleges in total) are shown in table 15. Once again the totals did not always correspond exactly with the totals implied in the previous section for FEFC-funded additional support (table 12, final column, for example), but once again, considerable effort has been made in dialogue with many colleges to reduce the inconsistencies between the different sets of data. As a result, the remaining differences

are now of a sufficiently small order of magnitude to be confident that table 15 provides a broad indication of the total breakdown of additional support by the various funding categories.

73   Table A25 (in appendix 1) shows how the patterns of funding claimed under the FEFC's additional support bands varied between institution types. Generally speaking, tertiary colleges, general further education colleges and agriculture and horticulture colleges had larger percentages of students in the higher bands (with 31%, 27% and 28% respectively in the bands over £2,000) than did sixth form colleges (23% in the higher bands) or art and design colleges (only 6% in these bands). This pattern is not unexpected, however, given the variation in the incidence of different types of disability between institution types recorded in chapter 3. Similarly, table A26 (in appendix

Table 15.   Students with learning difficulties and/or disabilities receiving FEFC-funded learning support through FEFC additional support bands

Annual cost for each student	Students in funding category		Average no. of students in each college
	No.	%	(N=249 colleges)
£170–£500	7,831	23.4	31.5
£501–£1,000	9,014	27.0	36.2
£1,001–£2,000	7,494	22.4	30.1
£2,001–£4,000	5,776	17.3	23.2
£4,001–£5,600	1,963	5.9	7.9
£5,601–£8,800	783	2.3	3.1
£8,801 and over	557	1.7	2.2
Total	**33,418**	**100.00**	**134.2**

1) shows that the smallest colleges tended to have the smallest share of students in the higher additional support bands.

Non-FEFC-funded learning support

74   Respondents were asked whether there were any students with learning difficulties and/or disabilities in their institution who were receiving learning support which is (wholly or partly) funded by non-FEFC sources[1]. Some 262 of the 274 colleges answered this question, and of these, over 183, or 70% responded that there were such students in their institution.

75   Table A27 (appendix 1) shows that the proportion of colleges with non-FEFC funded learning support was lowest among sixth form colleges (just over 36%), and highest among general further education colleges, art and design colleges, and agriculture and horticulture colleges (over 80% in each case). Smaller colleges (those with fewer than 2,500 students) were also less reliant on non-FEFC sources than their larger counterparts (see table A29 in appendix 1), and there was some regional variation (table A28), from a low in Yorkshire and Humberside (where 53% of colleges reported use of non-FEFC funded learning support) to a high in the South West (where the corresponding figure was 88%).

76   Those colleges which reported that they had students whose learning support was not funded by the FEFC were asked to identify the sources of funding for such learning support, and the responses from those able to identify the source(s) in question (179 colleges in all) are summarised in figure 6. It can be seen that the dominant source was the college's own internal budget (much of which will be ultimately sourced from the FEFC, even if the funding has not been earmarked for additional support). The next largest source, unsurprisingly, was the relevant local education authority (LEA), followed by training and enterprise council (TEC) funding. Tables A31 and A32 (in

appendix 1) show that there was some variation in these patterns by institution type and college size, with sixth form colleges, and art and design colleges most reliant on internal funds, whilst tertiary and general further education colleges drew more heavily on the local education authority. TEC funding was most heavily used by agriculture and horticulture colleges (and least by sixth form colleges). The size patterns are less clear, although there is some tendency for the largest colleges to make greater use of all of the non-FEFC sources identified.

Figure 6. Non-FEFC sources of additional support funding

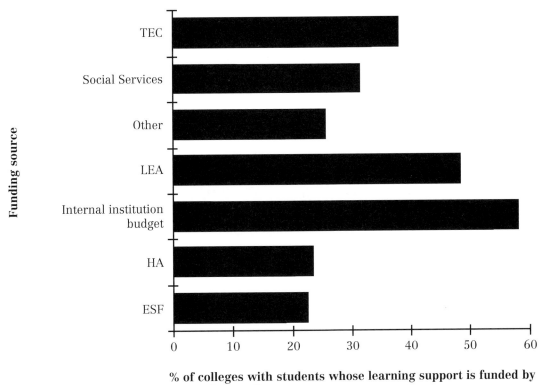

% of colleges with students whose learning support is funded by source in question

Source: appendix 1, table A30
Note: LEA = local education authority; TEC = training and enterprise council;
HA = health authority; ESF = European Social Fund

*Mapping Provision: The Provision of and Participation in Further Education by Students with Learning
Difficulties and/or Disabilities*

ENDNOTES

1 Throughout this section, and in the corresponding tables in appendix 1 (tables A27 to A32) we refer to learning support funded other than through the FEFC additional support arrangements/bands, as 'non-FEFC-funded learning support'. Clearly if, as the data suggest, some of this support is funded through colleges' own budgets, some of the relevant funding will also have originated from the FEFC via the recurrent funding methodology. The point here is that this latter was not part of any funding specifically allocated for additional learning support under the funding methodology.

38

Mapping Provision: The Provision of and Participation in Further Education by Students with Learning Difficulties and/or Disabilities

Unmet Need

· ·

Internal Unmet Need

77 The survey explored the issue of unmet need, and the extent to which a college was able (in the view of the respondents to the survey) to meet the learning support needs of students and potential students with learning difficulties and/or disabilities.

78 An analytical distinction was made in the survey between 'internal' and 'external' unmet need.

79 By 'internal' unmet need we mean the learning support needs of already enrolled students with learning difficulties and/or disabilities which the institution is unable to meet, or unable to meet in full; and by 'external' unmet need we mean the learning support needs of potential students with learning difficulties and/or disabilities, who are unable to participate in further education at the institution in question, because the institution is unable to meet these needs. Within this latter category, it is necessary to make a further distinction between:

- *expressed unmet need*: that is, non-participants who have expressed a wish to participate in further education, but who have been unable to participate, because of the nature of provision, access barriers, and;

- *unexpressed unmet need*: that is, non-participants who do not currently express a wish to participate in further education, but who might do so under appropriate circumstances. Considerable research with potential participants would be necessary to define these circumstances.

80 It should be stressed throughout that we are reporting *college perceptions* of unmet needs (of both types), and in the absence of external corroborative evidence (for example, from a survey of students or potential students), the data presented here should not be interpreted as representing definitive estimates of unmet need for further education among people with learning difficulties and/or disabilities. Rather they should be seen, at best, as preliminary indicators of the potential scale of unmet need, and of how it may be distributed across types of student, types of need and types of institution[1].

Identification of internal unmet need

81 Respondents were asked whether there were any enrolled students who had been identified as having learning support needs, and whose needs the institution was not able to meet or to meet in full (but excluding students who declined to take up the support offered by the institution). Table 16 summarises responses to this question.

Table 16. Existence of internal unmet need

Are there enrolled students with learning difficulties and/or disabilities whose learning support needs cannot be met (in full)?	Respondents	
	No.	%
Yes	80	30.0
No	166	62.2
Don't know	21	7.9
Total (N=100%)	**267**	**100.0**

39

82   Whilst nearly 63% of respondents did not feel that internal unmet need in this sense existed in their institutions, a significant minority (30%) were clear that it did. As table A33 (appendix 1) shows, higher proportions of general further education colleges (34%) and tertiary colleges (30%) identified internal unmet need than did the other types of college. Regional variation was particularly marked in this context (table A34 in appendix 1), with only 13% of colleges in the Northern Region reporting internal unmet need, as against nearly 46% in Greater London, at the other end of the scale. There was also a slight (but not uniform) tendency for the identification of internal unmet need to increase with college size (table A35 in appendix 1).

Extent of internal unmet need

83   Those colleges identifying internal unmet need were then asked, firstly, to indicate if possible, the number of enrolled students whose needs the institution had not been able to meet (or meet in full). Fifty-six of the 80 colleges indicating internal unmet need were able to make an estimate of the numbers of students affected, and between the 56 colleges a total of 1,654 such students were identified (an average of 30 for each college[2]).

Table 17.   Nature of internal unmet need

Nature of unmet need	Respondents No.	%
Basic skills/ESOL	16	21.1
Dyslexia	14	18.4
Visual impairment	11	14.5
Disability affecting mobility	9	11.8
Resources*	7	9.2
Mental health problems	7	9.2
Severe learning difficulties	5	6.6
Emotional/behavioural difficulties	5	6.6
Hearing impairment	5	6.6
On-course difficulties	5	6.6
Staffing[†]	4	5.3
Autism	3	3.9
Moderate learning difficulties	3	3.9
Profound/complex/severe disabilities and/or difficulties	2	2.6
Communication/speech problems	2	2.6
Medical needs	2	2.6
Other physical disability	2	2.6
Temporary disability after illness (such as brain injuries, heart transplants)	1	1.3
Multiple disabilities	1	1.3
Other	10	13.2
Total responding	**76**	**100.0**

* respondents cited issues which might more appropriately have been included in the response to the subsequent question (see table 18) relating to specialist equipment, resources, study aids, new technology

[†] these responses might more appropriately have been included in table 18, but covered issues around staff shortage (of trained staff, classroom assistants), and/or around lack of staff/external support with specialist expertise (for example, specialist teachers of the deaf, blind, dyslexic, interpreters, physiotherapists)

Nature and origin of internal unmet need

84 Secondly, this group of colleges was asked to list the nature (or origin) of the needs involved which the college had been unable to meet. Some 76 of the 80 colleges with internal unmet need answered the question. Some framed their responses in terms of the nature of the learning difficulty and/or disability giving rise to the unmet need, whilst others focused on the aspect of provision which meant they could not meet the need. The responses are summarised in table 17, from which it can be seen that internal unmet need arose from a wide range of sources (most common being basic skills or ESOL needs; or needs arising from dyslexia or visual impairment).

Reasons for internal unmet need

85 Thirdly, colleges identifying internal unmet needs were asked why it was not possible to meet these needs, and their responses are shown in table 18. Almost without exception, respondents couched their explanations in terms of resource constraints, whether financial, physical or human. Most common, cited by nearly 50% of the colleges, were staffing constraints — this was not simply a question of funding (although funding constraints were often relevant), but was often explained in terms of the non-availability of the specialist skills in question. Secondly (cited by over 39% of respondents) came physical resources (most often lack of equipment, or access constraints — such as to buildings). Significant proportions of this group of colleges mentioned funding constraints of one type or another.

External unmet need

86 By definition, the existence, nature and extent of external unmet need in the sense we have defined it is likely to be much harder for colleges to identify. The survey did, however, attempt to address this area with a number of questions.

Systems for recording expressed external unmet need

87 First, institutions were asked whether they had systems in place to record instances where potential students with a learning difficulty and/or disability apply to the institution, but could not be enrolled for any reason. Some 268 of the 274 colleges answered this question and, as can be seen from table 19, the majority (nearly 64%) reported that they did have such systems.

Table 18.   Reasons for internal unmet need

Reasons	Respondents	
	No.	%
Staffing (lack of trained personnel — internal or external — especially for deaf, blind and dyslexic students)	38	48.7
Resources (lack of/inadequate: resources; appropriate technology; equipment facilities; space; access; environment)	31	39.7
FEFC funding	17	21.8
Funding (general)	13	16.7
Internal funding	4	5.1
Other funding	2	2.6
Other	15	19.2
Total responding	**78**	**100.0**

Table 19. Systems for recording external unmet need

Can the college identify potential students with learning difficulties and/or disabilities who applied but could not be enrolled?	Respondents	
	No.	%
Yes	170	63.4
No	79	29.5
Don't know	19	7.1
Total (N=100%)	268	100.0

88   As tables A36 and A38 (in appendix 1) record, tertiary colleges and general further education colleges were much more likely than other types of college to have such systems in place, and larger colleges were generally more likely to have them than smaller colleges.

89   The colleges indicating that they did record these kinds of instances of external unmet need were asked to indicate how many such potential students there had been to date during the 1995-96 teaching year. Some 150 (out of 170) were able to make an estimate of the number, and the total number of students with learning difficulties and/or disabilities who had been thus 'turned away' at the time of the survey was 587 (an average of 3.9 for each college); and only a minority of colleges (42 or 28%) reported that there had been no such cases to date during the current teaching year. Not surprisingly (see tables A39 and A41 in appendix 1), general further education colleges, tertiary colleges, and larger colleges in general reported larger average numbers of potential students with learning difficulties and/or disabilities whose needs they were not able to meet.

Nature and origin of expressed external unmet need

90   These colleges were further asked to indicate the nature of the learning support needs involved, and the reasons why it was not possible to meet them, and their responses are summarised in tables 20 and 21.

91   There are, in tables 20 and 21, both similarities to and differences from the explanations given for internal unmet need (paragraph 85). Of particular note, when it comes to external unmet need, is the predominance of so-called 'non-educational needs[3]' in hampering colleges' ability to enrol some students with learning difficulties and/or disabilities. This category covered a multitude of factors, but common examples include students requiring support such as transport, 24-hour or residential care, personal care needs, as well as some instances where it was judged that the potential students had a demand for day-care services rather than education.

92   Looking at specific disability types whose needs could not be met, disabilities affecting mobility top the list (issues here focused on physical access), followed by profound or complex disabilities. In explaining the reasons for their inability to meet such needs (table 21), colleges cited most commonly physical resource constraints (including availability of specialist equipment), followed by staffing or personnel constraints.

Role of other local providers in meeting external unmet need

93   Clearly, the extent to which a college's ability or inability to provide for a particular need has an impact upon participation rates is also dependent on whether and to what extent other local providers or institutions are able to meet the need in question. Colleges

Table 20.   Nature of external unmet need

Nature of unmet need	Respondents	
	No.	%
Disability affecting mobility	40	31.5
Non-educational needs	34	26.8
Profound/complex/severe learning difficulties and/or disabilities	23	18.1
Visual impairment	22	17.3
Severe learning difficulties	16	12.6
Hearing impairment	15	11.8
Emotional/behavioural difficulties	12	9.4
Other	10	7.9
Multiple disabilities	8	6.3
Mental health problems	6	4.7
Medical needs	5	3.9
Other physical disability	4	3.1
Dyslexia	3	2.4
Moderate learning difficulties	3	2.4
Communication/speech problems	2	1.6
Basic skills/ESOL	2	1.6
Autism	1	0.8
Total responding	**127**	**100.0**

Table 21.   Reasons for external unmet need

Reason for unmet need	Respondents	
	No.	%
Resources	63	52.1
Non-educational needs	51	42.1
Staffing	29	24.0
Lack appropriate course/level of study	16	13.2
Funding (general)	5	4.1
FEFC funding	3	2.5
Late application	3	2.5
Other funding	2	1.7
Internal funding	1	0.8
Other	10	8.3
Total responding	**121**	**100.0**

indicating that they were aware of external unmet needs were also asked, therefore, whether other local providers were able to meet these needs. Of 132 colleges identifying external unmet need which answered this question, fewer than 58 (44%) felt that such needs were being met by other local providers, 48 (36%) felt that they were not, and the remainder (26 or 20%) were not sure.

94   There was some variation in institution type in response to this question (see table A42 in appendix 1) with sixth form colleges being the most sanguine that the needs they were unable to meet could be met by other local providers. Considerable regional variation was also evident (table A43) with, at one end of the scale, only 27% of colleges in the West Midlands region believing that other local providers could satisfy this unmet need compared, at the other end of the scale, with 67% of colleges in Greater London and the Northern Region. It was not possible, within the scope of this research exercise, to undertake detailed analysis of local catchment areas (and the relative location of alternative providers both within and outside

the sector) to try and explain these regional patterns, but it is clear that the matter is a more complex one than a simple question of urban–rural differences or college densities. Thus, whilst it is perhaps not surprising that Greater London colleges were more likely to see alternative sources in the locality to satisfy unmet need, the differences between some of the other regions is much harder to explain.

95   Those 58 colleges indicating that other local providers meet the needs in question were asked to specify which local providers these were, and the answers from the 56 who responded are summarised in figure 7.

Identification of local unexpressed demand for further education

96   Finally, in the context of unmet need, colleges were asked whether their institution had any way, in general, of identifying the potential, but currently unexpressed demand for participation in further education among people with learning difficulties and/or disabilities within the local population. Table 22 shows their responses to this question.

Figure 7.   Local providers meeting learning support needs which respondent colleges could not

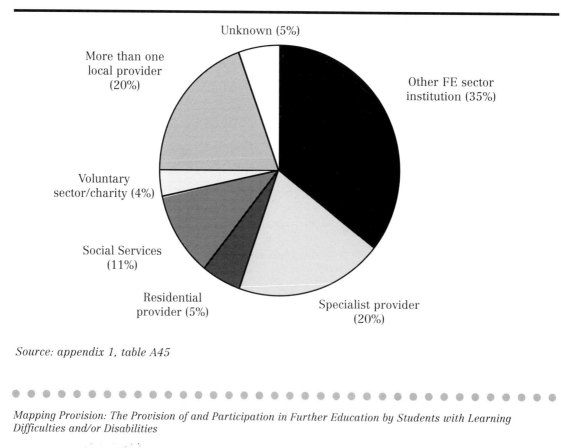

Source: appendix 1, table A45

Mapping Provision: The Provision of and Participation in Further Education by Students with Learning Difficulties and/or Disabilities

97 Perhaps surprisingly (at least in the light of the earlier pilot stages of the research which indicated considerable pessimism on this front), some 66% of responding colleges claimed to be able to identify such unexpressed demand (and this varied from a low of 44% in sixth form colleges to a high of 85% in tertiary colleges; see table A46 in appendix 1). Larger colleges were also clearly much more confident in identifying unexpressed demand than were smaller colleges (see table A48 in appendix 1)

98 These colleges were then asked to estimate the number of such potential students with learning difficulties and/or disabilities for each year in their catchment areas. Some 77 colleges (less than 50%) were able to provide estimates, but the numbers involved were considerable — 23,872 students in total, representing an average of 310 for each college[4].

99 If we put this information together with that on the size of the existing student population with learning difficulties and/or disabilities (for the same colleges providing both sets of information, that is, 76 in total), this suggests that the perceived potential student population with learning difficulties and/or disabilities could be almost double the existing numbers (the combined enrolled student population with learning difficulties and/or disabilities in the 76 colleges is currently 26,055 compared with an estimate of unexpressed local demand of 23,842[5]).

100 Finally, the 176 colleges which claimed to be able to identify unexpressed demand for participation in further education were asked to indicate which information source(s) they used to contribute to identifying such demand (table 23). Most notable from table 23, perhaps, is the strong reliance on contact with other relevant organisations, and the relative under-use of formal statistical sources (either in the form of college-generated surveys and research, or the use of external demographic statistics).

101 The survey reinforced the earlier findings from the pilot stages of the research, namely that for the most part, colleges' use of external information sources to estimate demand tended to be *ad hoc*, somewhat unsystematic, and heavily dependent on local institutional networks (both formal and informal). It is clearly very common, for example, to use information from local schools, local education authorities and health authorities to assess the level of potential demand from people with learning difficulties and/or disabilities. There was no evidence from the survey, however, that colleges had been able to integrate data from these different sources to build up a systematic picture of their local catchment areas, and there is a clear need implied by these results for the development of a methodology that colleges can use to systematise and integrate the many data sources they currently use[6].

Table 22. Identifying potential but currently unexpressed demand

Can college identify potential demand for FE among local population with learning difficulties and/or disabilities?	Respondents	
	No.	%
Yes	175	66.8
No	74	28.2
Don't know	13	5.0
Total (N=100%)	**262**	**100.0**

Table 23. Information sources used to identify potential but currently unexpressed demand

Source	Respondents	
	No.	*%*
Formal links with schools	165	93.8
Careers service	153	86.9
Social/health services	148	84.1
Informal contacts	146	83.0
Voluntary organisation(s)	107	60.8
Community outreach work	93	52.8
Institution needs analysis/marketing	80	45.5
Own survey/research	58	33.9
Local/regional statistics (for example, census and other demographic information)	50	28.4
Other	35	19.9
Total responding (N=100%)	**176**	**100.0**

102 The survey and pilot interviews also suggested that occasionally small local surveys have been conducted by colleges, of an area or of local schools for example. Again, however, the extent to which this type of information is regularly or systematically collected is extremely limited. It is also worth noting that some comments were made by survey respondents which suggested that the incorporation of colleges might have reduced the extent to which this type of information is collected and utilised in a local area. Now that colleges are in competition, it was argued, there tended to be less communication between them and less sharing of information on demand, unmet need and the like (despite the fact that their provision might often be complementary — what one college cannot provide, another perhaps can).

ENDNOTES

1 Some of the difficulties inherent in estimating unmet need from a college survey are mentioned in chapter 1.

2 The median value was, however, much lower at six students for each college, indicating that the average is skewed upwards by a small number of colleges reporting a large number of such students with unmet need. Individual colleges reported numbers varying between a low of one student, and a high of 1,654 enrolled students whose needs could not be met.

3 It should be stressed that this terminology is not ours, but that of a number of our respondents, who used the term 'non-educational needs' to refer to what are sometimes denoted 'prior and associated needs'.

4 Once again, the median value at 50 potential students for each college was much lower than the mean, reflecting the influence of a few colleges making very high estimates. The actual numbers given by colleges in response to this question varied from a low of zero to a high of 5,239 potential students.

5 Too few colleges provided such estimates for further breakdowns by college type, region or size to be statistically reliable.

6 It is likely that the proposed work to be commissioned by the FEFC's learning difficulties and/or disabilities and widening participation committees to develop a practical guide for colleges to map their local population and conduct their needs analyses, will go some way towards remedying this deficiency.

47

Mapping Provision: The Provision of and Participation in Further Education by Students with Learning Difficulties and/or Disabilities

Colleges' Overall Approach to Provision for Students with Learning Difficulties and/or Disabilities

Approach to Provision

103 In order to gain a picture of colleges' overall approach to provision for students with learning difficulties and/or disabilities, and how this approach varied by college type, respondents were asked to indicate the extent to which they agreed or disagreed with each of a series of statements about their approach to provision. Their responses are summarised in table 24.

104 There was a very strong clustering of these responses, with the vast majority of respondents declaring that they have an inclusive, open-access approach, with cross-institution learning support provision, and widespread assessment of most or all students. Further breakdown of the responses suggested, however, that there was some variation between institution types. Thus, table A49 (in appendix 1) indicates that this kind of approach — open access, cross-institution learning support, specialist learning support staff — is most prevalent in general further education colleges, tertiary colleges, and art and design colleges, and less prevalent particularly in sixth form colleges, (although the data also suggest that sixth form colleges are least likely have a policy based on offering 'discrete' provision to students with learning difficulties and/or disabilities). This

result is consistent with findings reported earlier (see paragraphs 45 to 48).

105 Some similar variation by college size in overall approach was also evident (see table A50 in appendix 1), with larger colleges more likely to have an open-access approach, more likely to employ specialist learning support staff, less likely only to offer 'discrete' provision.

106 Of most interest, however, is to discover whether there is any relationship between the overall approach or strategy claimed by the institution, and its provision in practice. Perhaps the clearest way of examining this is to look for a relationship between the stated strategy and the extent to which there are students with learning difficulties and/or disabilities participating in the institution in question. Table 25 does this, by relating colleges' average scores on the five-point agreement scale for each of the statements in the survey about overall approach to provision, to the proportion of enrolled students in the colleges in question. Reassuringly, there is a clear relationship in the anticipated direction, although it is not always a strong one. Thus, in general terms, colleges which claim to have open access, a cross-institution approach to learning support, specialist learning support staff, and a comprehensive approach to assessment, tend (on average)

Table 24. Overall approach to provision for students with learning difficulties and/or disabilities

Statement	Respondents					Average	N=100%
	Strongly agree	Agree	Neither agree nor disagree	Disagree	Strongly disagree		
	(1)	(2)	(3)	(4)	(5)		
There is a cross-institution approach to learning support	128	115	20	8	1	1.7	272
The institution has a policy of 'open access' to all potential students irrespective of learning difficulty and/or disability	115	109	20	27	2	1.9	273
The institution employs specialist learning support staff who meet most learning support needs	102	120	20	23	5	1.9	270
All students are assessed for learning support needs	58	98	43	55	14	2.5	268
Learning support is mostly provided by lecturing/tutorial staff	54	85	58	63	8	2.6	268
The main provision for students with learning difficulties and/or disabilities is on 'discrete' courses	15	62	43	65	83	3.5	268
Students are assessed for learning support only if self-identified, or on the basis of prior information	16	37	16	116	81	3.8	266

also to have higher participation rates of students with learning difficulties and/or disabilities.

107 These results suggest, at the very least, that colleges' overall approaches do appear to be associated with practices. Whilst this is, on the face of it, encouraging, we would nevertheless urge some caution in making strong statements about the direction and degree of causality involved. We must, in particular, allow for the possibility that some of this association is a 'recording effect' and that colleges with open, inclusive, approaches with widespread assessment may record higher levels of participation, simply because they are more likely to identify learning difficulties and/or disabilities and associated support needs among their students.

50

Mapping Provision: The Provision of and Participation in Further Education by Students with Learning Difficulties and/or Disabilities

Table 25.   Overall approach to provision for students with learning difficulties and/or disabilities, by share of enrolled students with learning difficulties and/or disabilities

Statement	Average score for each statement (1 = 'strongly agree' ... 5 = 'strongly disagree')		
	Share of S* less than 3.5%	Share of S* between 3.5% and 5.9%	Share of S* 6.0% or more
There is a cross-institution approach to learning support	1.8	1.6	1.6
The institution has a policy of 'open access' to all potential students irrespective of learning difficulty and/or disability	2.1	1.7	1.8
The institution employs specialist learning support staff who meet most learning support needs	2.2	1.7	1.8
All students are assessed for learning support needs	2.5	2.7	2.3
Learning support is mostly provided by lecturing/tutorial staff	2.3	2.7	2.7
The main provision for students with learning difficulties and/or disabilities is on 'discrete' courses	3.6	3.4	3.5
Students are assessed for learning support only if self-identified, or on the basis of prior information	3.7	3.8	4.0

Note: S = students with learning difficulties and/or disabilities*

Appendices

Statistical Tables from the College Survey

Table A1. Share of students with learning difficulties and/or disabilities by type of institution

Institution type	Enrolled students with learning difficulties and/or disabilities	Respondent institutions
	%	No.
Agriculture and horticulture college	8.2	18
Art and design college	5.7	7
General further education college	5.8	138
Sixth form college	5.6	66
Specialist designated institution	1.4	7
Tertiary college	5.4	36
Total (N=100%)	**5.7**	**272**

Table A2. Share of students with learning difficulties and/or disabilities by FEFC region

FEFC region	Enrolled students with learning difficulties and/or disabilities	Respondents
	%	No.
East Midlands	5.5	20
Eastern Region	6.1	28
Greater London	3.4	34
North West	5.9	35
Northern Region	4.7	15
South East	4.8	35
South West	5.3	26
West Midlands	7.8	45
Yorkshire and Humberside	6.5	34
Total (N=100%)	**5.7**	**272**

Table A3. Share of students with learning difficulties and/or disabilities by size of college

Enrolled students	Enrolled students with learning difficulties and/or disabilities	Respondents
	%	No.
0–999	7.4	43
1,000–2,499	5.9	57
2,500–4,999	5.6	43
5,000–7,499	5.7	60
7,500 or more	4.9	69
Total (N=100%)	**5.7**	**272**

Note: college size as at November 1994

Table A4. Variation in size of surveyed colleges by FEFC region

FEFC region	Enrolled students Average No.	Respondents No.
East Midlands	3,991	20
Eastern Region	6,208	28
Greater London	5,727	36
North West	7,189	35
Northern Region	4,183	15
South East	4,199	35
South West	4,889	26
West Midlands	4,572	45
Yorkshire and Humberside	5,780	34
Total (N=100%)	**5,294**	**274**

Note: average number of enrolled students as at November 1994

Table A5. Share of part-time students with learning difficulties and/or disabilities by type of institution

Institution type	Responses		Overall student population data (for respondents)	
	Part-time students with learning difficulties and/ or disabilities %	Respondents No.	Overall enrolled part-time student population %	Respondents No.
Agriculture and horticulture college	48.7	18	65.2	18
Art and design college	31.3	6	48.3	7
General further education college	58.7	133	70.7	138
Specialist designated institution	86.5	7	98.1	7
Sixth form college	14.4	64	22.7	66
Tertiary college	54.3	34	69.3	36
Total (N=100%)	**55.0**	**262**	**67.9**	**272**

Table A6. Share of part-time students with learning difficulties and/or disabilities by FEFC region

FEFC region	Responses		Overall student population data (for responding colleges)	
	Part-time students with learning difficulties and /or disabilities	Respondents	Overall enrolled part-time student population	Respondents
	%	No.	%	No.
East Midlands	53.1	19	71.2	20
Eastern Region	57.0	28	67.6	28
Greater London	50.9	32	66.2	34
North West	52.3	33	72.8	35
Northern Region	52.6	15	65.3	15
South East	40.1	35	62.6	35
South West	54.3	22	67.3	26
West Midlands	57.7	45	65.6	45
Yorkshire and Humberside	64.7	32	69.7	34
Total (N=100%)	**55.0**	**261**	**67.9**	**272**

Table A7. Share of part-time students with learning difficulties and/or disabilities by college size

Enrolled students	Responses		Overall student population data (for responding colleges)	
	Part-time students with learning difficulties and /or disabilities	Respondents	Overall enrolled part-time student population	Respondents
	%	No.	%	No.
0–999	22.4	43	28.8	43
1,000–2,499	18.5	54	34.7	57
2,500–4,999	56.6	43	66.3	43
5,000–7,499	53.3	56	67.2	60
7,500–9,999	58.7	28	72.9	28
10,000 or more	62.0	38	74.0	41
Total (N=100%)	**55.0**	**262**	**67.9**	**272**

Note: college size as at November 1994

Appendix 1

Table A8. Sex and age distribution of students with learning difficulties and/or disabilities by type of institution

Institution type	Sex		Students with learning difficulties and/or disabilities aged			
	Female students with learning difficulties and /or disabilities %	N=	16–18 %	19–24 %	25+ %	N=
Agriculture and horticulture college	43.7	17	44.0	18.8	37.2	15
Art and design college	39.7	5	53.6	25.5	20.9	5
General further education college	49.6	128	28.2	17.6	54.3	147
Specialist designated institution	55.1	7	0.0	17.6	82.4	7
Sixth form college	47.6	63	82.7	4.4	12.9	63
Tertiary college	48.9	32	34.3	14.7	51.0	32
Total (N=100%)	**49.2**	**252**	**31.3**	**17.9**	**49.2**	**249**

Table A9. Sex and age distribution of students with learning difficulties and/or disabilities by FEFC region

FEFC region	Sex		Students with learning difficulties and/or disabilities aged			
	Female students with learning difficulties and/ or disabilities %	N=	16–18 %	19–24 %	25+ %	N=
East Midlands	50.7	18	37.5	16.8	45.7	18
Eastern Region	51.9	26	37.7	15.3	46.9	27
Greater London	48.3	31	35.7	21.7	42.7	31
North West	49.6	33	18.1	14.0	68.0	32
Northern Region	44.9	15	42.3	18.2	39.5	14
South East	46.0	35	56.9	14.4	28.7	34
South West	47.6	22	34.4	17.6	48.0	21
West Midlands	50.7	45	33.0	17.5	49.4	43
Yorkshire and Humberside	48.3	27	25.2	15.8	58.9	29
Total (N=100%)	**49.2**	**252**	**31.3**	**17.9**	**49.2**	**249**

Table A10. Sex and age distribution of students with learning difficulties and/or disabilities by college size

Enrolled students	Sex		Students with learning difficulties and/or disabilities aged			
	Female students with learning difficulties and /or disabilities %	N=	16–18 %	19–24 %	25+ %	N=
0–999	43.7	43	68.5	13.6	17.9	42
1,000–2,499	46.4	50	79.2	7.4	13.4	50
2,500–4,999	49.7	43	36.6	16.4	47.0	41
5,000–7,499	48.5	53	38.7	17.0	44.2	54
7,500–9,999	46.4	28	30.4	21.1	48.5	28
10,000 or more	51.3	35	20.0	16.0	64.0	34
Total (N=100%)	**49.2**	**252**	**31.3**	**17.9**	**49.2**	**249**

Note: college size as at November 1994

Table A11. Ethnic origin of students with learning difficulties and/or disabilities by type of institution

Institution type	Students with learning difficulties and/or disabilities who are			
	White %	Non-white %	of unknown ethnic origin %	N=
Agriculture and horticulture college	97.9	1.1	1.0	17
Art and design college	98.7	0.8	0.4	5
General further education college	80.7	8.9	10.4	125
Sixth form college	77.4	9.4	13.2	63
Specialist designated institution	43.4	54.3	2.3	7
Tertiary college	74.3	10.7	15.0	31
Total (N=100%)	**79.8**	**9.3**	**10.9**	**248**

59

Mapping Provision: The Provision of and Participation in Further Education by Students with Learning Difficulties and/or Disabilities

Appendix 1

Table A12. Ethnic origin of students with learning difficulties and/or disabilities by FEFC region

FEFC Region	Students with learning difficulties and/or disabilities who are			
	White	Non-white	of unknown ethnic origin	N=
	%	%	%	
East Midlands	79.0	10.2	10.9	18
Eastern Region	75.9	6.5	17.7	26
Greater London	48.1	39.8	12.1	29
North West	86.7	3.6	9.7	31
Northern Region	90.5	2.5	7.0	15
South East	87.1	4.4	8.5	34
South West	87.7	1.3	11.0	22
West Midlands	75.1	11.5	13.4	45
Yorkshire and Humberside	86.6	10.0	3.4	28
Total (N=100%)	**79.8**	**9.3**	**10.9**	**248**

Table A13. Ethnic origin of students with learning difficulties and/or disabilities by college size

Enrolled students	Students with learning difficulties and/or disabilities who are			
	White	Non-white	of unknown ethnic origin	N=
	%	%	%	
0–999	90.4	8.0	1.5	43
1,000–2,499	81.7	9.5	8.7	51
2,500–4,999	77.5	9.5	13.0	41
5,000–7,499	81.1	7.3	11.6	55
7,500–9,999	80.4	9.7	10.0	26
10,000 or more	78.5	10.3	11.2	32
Total (N=100%)	**79.8**	**9.3**	**10.9**	**248**

Note: college size as at November 1994

Mapping Provision: The Provision of and Participation in Further Education by Students with Learning Difficulties and/or Disabilities

Table A14. Type of learning programme followed by students with learning difficulties and/or disabilities by type of institution

Institution type	Students with learning difficulties and/or disabilities following programmes of type			
	a) programme designed for any student	b) programme designed solely/ primarily for students with learning difficulties and/or disabilities	c) programme combining elements of a) and b)	N=
	%	%	%	
Agriculture and horticulture college	64.1	24.9	10.9	18
Art and design college	82.6	13.6	3.8	7
General further education college	50.4	45.8	3.7	125
Sixth form college	79.9	13.5	7.6	63
Specialist designated institution	24.9	75.1	0.0	7
Tertiary college	50.5	44.9	4.7	34
Total (N=100%)	**52.8**	**42.9**	**4.3**	**254**

Table A15. Type of learning programme followed by students with learning difficulties and/or disabilities by FEFC region

FEFC region	Students with learning difficulties and/or disabilities following programmes of type			
	a) programme designed for any student	b) programme designed solely/ primarily for students with learning difficulties and/or disabilities	c) programme combining elements of a) and b)	N=
	%	%	%	
East Midlands	57.2	33.1	9.7	18
Eastern Region	47.1	52.9	4.2	26
Greater London	47.6	49.2	3.1	31
North West	64.9	31.2	3.9	32
Northern Region	64.7	29.9	5.4	15
South East	53.4	43.8	2.8	34
South West	57.9	39.7	2.5	24
West Midlands	47.7	47.2	5.1	42
Yorkshire and Humberside	47.9	47.6	4.6	32
Total (N=100%)	**52.8**	**42.9**	**4.6**	**254**

Appendix 1

Table A16. Type of learning programme followed by students with learning difficulties and/or disabilities by college size

Enrolled students	*Students with learning difficulties and/or disabilities following programmes of type*			
	a) programme designed for any student	*b) programme designed solely/ primarily for students with learning difficulties and/or disabilities*	*c) programme combining elements of a) and b)*	*N=*
	%	%	%	
0–999	83.3	13.3	3.5	43
1,000–2,499	69.1	20.1	10.8	54
2,500–4,999	46.1	48.6	5.3	39
5,000–7,499	54.2	41.3	4.5	55
7,500–9,999	44.0	52.6	3.5	27
10,000 or more	51.2	45.6	3.2	36
Total (N=100%)	**52.8**	**42.9**	**4.3**	**254**

Note: college size as at November 1994

Table A17. Level of learning programme followed by students with learning difficulties and/or disabilities

Level of learning programme	*Students with learning difficulties and/or disabilities in respondent institutions following programme*	
	No.	%
Pre-vocational/foundation	30,105	46.9
(G)NVQ Level 1 or equivalent	10,459	16.3
(G)NVQ Level 2 or equivalent — including GCSEs	12,483	19.5
(G)NVQ Level 3 or equivalent — including GCE A/AS level	9,326	14.5
(G)NVQ Level 4 or equivalent	856	1.3
Other/non-vocational courses*	901	1.4
Total (N=100%)	**64,130**	**100.0**

* this category was not included in the survey question since in principle the other five categories cover all levels of provision likely to be encountered. In practice, however, a small number of respondents 'wrote in' further categories which they did not believe were covered by the survey definitions. Where possible these entries have been recoded to the appropriate categories. Where this was not possible, however (for example, because the respondent wrote in 'other'), the students in question are included in this residual category

Note: based on 241 institutions

Table A18. Level of learning programme followed by students with learning difficulties and/or disabilities by type of institution

Institution type	Students with learning difficulties and/or disabilities following programmes of level		
	Pre-vocational/foundation	(G)NVQ level 3 or 4 or equivalent	N=
	%	%	
Agriculture and horticulture college	26.1	18.1	18
Art and design college	5.0	78.7	5
General further education college	48.5	12.2	118
Sixth form college	16.0	54.2	61
Specialist designated institution	0.3	11.0	7
Tertiary college	58.0	12.9	32
Total (N=100%)	**46.9**	**15.8**	**241**

Table A19. Level of learning programme followed by students with learning difficulties and/or disabilities by FEFC region

FEFC region	Students with learning difficulties and/or disabilities following programmes of level		
	Pre-vocational/foundation	(G)NVQ level 3 or 4 or equivalent	N=
	%	%	
East Midlands	38.2	12.2	16
Eastern Region	48.3	15.1	27
Greater London	45.4	16.7	30
North West	39.0	19.4	28
Northern Region	44.0	15.9	13
South East	31.7	27.7	32
South West	44.3	19.9	21
West Midlands	52.4	10.0	44
Yorkshire and Humberside	58.6	11.7	30
Total (N=100%)	**46.9**	**15.8**	**241**

Appendix 1

Table A20. Level of learning programme followed by students with learning difficulties and/or disabilities by college size

Enrolled students	Students with learning difficulties and/or disabilities following programmes of level		
	Pre-vocational/foundation	(G)NVQ level 3 or 4 or equivalent	N=
	%	%	
0–999	11.1	47.2	43
1,000–2,499	22.1	45.4	50
2,500–4,999	56.7	13.6	42
5,000–7,499	41.4	13.0	55
7,500–9,999	51.0	12.4	25
10,000 or more	54.3	10.8	26
Total (N=100%)	**46.9**	**15.8**	**241**

Note: college size as at November 1994

Table A21. Incidence of different types of learning difficulty and/or disability by type of institution

Learning difficulty and/or disability	Students with characteristic in question					
	Sixth form	Tertiary	Art & design	Gen FE	Agric/hort	Specialist designated
	%	%	%	%	%	%
Moderate learning difficulties	13.4	22.7	2.1	22.4	39.7	16.7
Severe learning difficulties	1.7	19.5	15.2	17.3	10.5	0.0
Unspecified/unknown	1.8	7.9	0.0	9.1	2.9	0.7
Specific learning difficulties	41.8	12.6	43.5	9.2	14.3	43.1
Other medical condition	12.9	5.8	24.2	6.4	3.4	0.7
Multiple disabilities	4.2	6.5	0.8	8.7	3.5	4.9
Mental ill health	0.7	1.8	2.3	3.5	1.9	0.0
Hearing impairment	5.7	4.6	8.1	4.1	1.9	11.4
Disability affecting mobility	2.5	4.5	2.2	4.4	2.1	18.8
Basic skills/ESOL needs	4.9	4.4	0.0	2.7	14.5	0.0
Visual impairment	3.2	2.8	0.7	3.6	0.8	2.4
Other physical disability	2.8	1.9	0.1	2.5	1.1	1.4
Emotional/behavioural difficulties	2.2	2.2	0.0	2.1	2.6	0.0
Other	1.2	1.3	0.1	1.3	0.1	0.0
Profound/complex disabilities	0.1	1.1	0.0	1.6	0.3	0.0
Temporary disability after illness/accident	0.6	0.3	0.7	0.4	0.5	0.0
Total (no. of respondents =)	**65**	**35**	**7**	**138**	**18**	**6**

Note: based on average percentage across colleges of each type

64

Mapping Provision: The Provision of and Participation in Further Education by Students with Learning Difficulties and/or Disabilities

Table A22. Incidence of different types of learning difficulty and/or disability by college size

Learning difficulty and/or disability	Students with characteristic in question					
	0–999	1,000 – 2,499	2,500 – 4,999	5,000 – 7,499	7,500 – 9,999	10,000 or more
	%	%	%	%	%	%
Moderate learning difficulties	19.5	14.8	24.5	26.6	18.8	19.2
Severe learning difficulties	4.1	6.0	20.9	14.4	20.7	16.3
Unspecified/unknown	0.8	2.7	9.6	7.8	6.4	12.1
Specific learning difficulties	35.9	36.9	7.9	10.4	11.4	9.1
Other medical condition	12.5	9.5	6.9	8.1	5.2	4.6
Multiple disabilities	4.1	6.4	9.8	7.2	8.6	4.1
Mental ill health	1.1	1.1	1.6	2.1	3.2	6.1
Hearing impairment	5.4	4.8	4.3	3.9	4.4	5.6
Disability affecting mobility	4.1	2.7	3.6	3.7	4.3	6.9
Basic skills/ESOL need	4.4	7.9	1.5	4.0	3.0	2.1
Visual impairment	2.8	1.5	3.4	3.9	3.7	3.9
Other physical disability	2.0	1.8	1.6	2.6	2.4	3.7
Emotional/behavioural difficulties	1.9	1.9	1.6	2.5	1.8	2.4
Other	0.1	1.4	0.5	1.0	2.7	1.7
Profound/complex disabilities	0.4	0.1	1.5	1.1	3.1	0.7
Temporary disability after illness/accident	0.7	0.4	0.5	0.3	0.3	0.4
Total (no. of respondents =)	42	57	43	60	28	39

Note: based on average percentage across colleges of each type; college size as at November 1994

Appendix 1

Table A23. Nature of learning support provision offered by type of institution

Nature of support/ provision	Colleges of each type with students receiving support/ provision in question					
	Sixth form %	Tertiary %	Art & design %	Gen FE %	Agric/hort %	Specialist designated %
Support assistants (non-teaching)	43.9	94.4	71.4	96.4	61.1	14.3
Supplementary teaching (outside main course)	65.2	75.0	57.1	77.1	77.8	28.6
Specialist equipment	42.4	80.6	42.9	82.1	38.9	42.9
Specialist assessment	43.9	69.4	57.1	81.4	61.1	28.6
Communicators/specialist teaching (for hearing impaired students)	34.8	75.0	85.7	82.1	50.0	0.0
Drop-in support centres (for example, basic skills workshops)	36.4	77.8	14.3	74.3	66.7	28.6
Specialist careers advice	33.3	69.4	14.3	71.4	44.4	14.3
Educational psychology	47.0	80.6	28.6	61.4	27.8	0.0
Transport between home and the institution	31.8	75.0	14.3	66.4	44.4	0.0
Class support from additional teacher	24.2	69.4	14.3	67.9	50.0	28.6
Cross-institution learning support team(s)	30.3	66.7	14.3	65.7	38.9	0.0
Specialist teaching for blind/partially-sighted students	21.2	58.3	0.0	57.9	16.7	14.3
Social work support	25.8	30.6	14.3	52.9	44.4	0.0
Transport between sites	7.6	52.8	28.6	54.3	27.8	0.0
Taping/brailling	10.6	44.4	14.3	49.3	16.7	28.6
Speech/communication/ language therapy	10.6	27.8	0.0	39.3	16.7	0.0
Specialist counselling for disabled people	10.6	30.6	0.0	30.7	5.6	0.0
Nursing support/medical services	6.1	25.0	0.0	28.6	11.1	0.0
Specialist psychiatric support	7.6	11.1	14.3	30.7	11.1	0.0
Physiotherapy	12.1	16.7	0.0	20.0	5.6	0.0
Total (no. of respondents =)	66	36	7	140	18	7

Table A24. Nature of learning support provision offered by college size

Nature of support/ provision	Enrolled students receiving support/provision in question					
	0–999	1,000 – 2,499	2,500 – 4,999	5,000 – 7,499	7,500 – 9,999	10,000 or more
	%	%	%	%	%	%
Support assistants (non-teaching)	34.9	59.6	93.2	96.7	100.0	92.7
Supplementary teaching (outside main course)	60.5	75.4	72.7	70.5	89.3	70.7
Specialist equipment	39.5	43.9	68.2	86.9	92.9	82.9
Specialist assessment	48.8	47.4	75.0	77.0	78.6	85.4
Communicators/specialist teaching (for hearing impaired students)	32.6	43.9	70.5	80.3	89.3	87.8
Drop-in support centres (for example, basic skills workshops)	44.2	36.8	75.0	77.0	85.7	65.9
Specialist careers advice	30.2	35.1	63.6	68.9	89.3	70.7
Educational psychology	30.2	49.1	43.2	72.1	78.6	65.9
Transport between home and the institution	25.6	38.6	59.1	65.6	78.6	70.7
Class support from additional teacher	23.3	29.8	54.5	72.1	75.0	78.0
Cross-institution learning support team(s)	27.9	33.3	52.3	72.1	64.3	68.3
Specialist teaching for blind/partially-sighted students	11.6	21.1	54.5	60.7	53.6	65.9
Social work support	25.6	22.8	50.0	44.3	57.1	53.7
Transport between sites	16.3	10.5	38.6	45.9	75.0	68.3
Taping/brailling	11.6	14.0	34.1	47.5	53.6	63.4
Speech/communication/ language therapy	7.0	17.5	29.5	37.7	39.3	36.6
Specialist counselling for disabled people	2.3	12.3	15.9	36.1	28.6	41.5
Nursing support/medical services	4.7	8.8	25.0	24.6	32.1	31.7
Specialist psychiatric support	4.7	10.5	18.2	24.6	35.7	34.1
Physiotherapy	9.3	8.8	18.2	19.7	25.0	17.1
Total (no. of respondents =)	**43**	**57**	**44**	**61**	**28**	**41**

Note: college size as at November 1994

Table A25. Students with learning difficulties and/or disabilities receiving learning support funded through FEFC additional support bands, by type of institution

Annual cost for each student	Students with learning difficulties and/or disabilities in funding category				
	Sixth form	Tertiary	Art & design	Gen FE	Agric/hort
	%	%	%	%	%
£170–£500	11.6	19.6	1.2	25.2	15.6
£501–£1,000	41.6	28.7	53.0	25.7	28.3
£1,001–£2,000	23.9	20.8	39.8	22.4	28.2
£2,001–£4,000	12.2	19.9	0.0	17.0	20.0
£4,001–£5,600	5.1	6.4	1.2	5.9	3.0
£5,601–£8,800	2.9	2.2	1.2	2.4	0.0
£8,801 and over	2.7	2.4	3.6	1.4	4.9
Total (no. of respondents =)	61	29	7	128	18

Note: no students in specialist designated institutions were reported as being supported through the FEFC's additional support bands

Table A26. Students with learning difficulties and/or disabilities receiving learning support funded through FEFC additional support bands, by college size

Annual cost for each student	Students with learning difficulties and/or disabilities in funding category					
	0–999	1,000 – 2,499	2,500 – 4,999	5,000 – 7,499	7,500 – 9,999	10,000 or more
	%	%	%	%	%	%
£170–£500	24.0	16.0	25.0	23.8	31.5	20.6
£501–£1,000	44.1	40.9	19.4	26.9	19.0	29.3
£1,001–£2,000	21.2	15.2	25.1	23.5	23.1	21.5
£2,001–£4,000	5.9	19.8	19.8	17.8	14.4	17.4
£4,001–£5,600	2.5	2.9	4.6	4.2	8.0	7.7
£5,601–£8,800	0.3	1.6	2.4	2.4	1.9	2.7
£8,801 and over	2.1	3.6	3.6	1.4	2.1	0.8
Total (no. of respondents =)	41	53	41	54	26	34

Table A27. Students with learning difficulties and/or disabilities receiving non-FEFC-funded learning support, by type of institution

Institution type	Colleges receiving non-FEFC-funded learning support	Respondents
	%	No.
Agriculture and horticulture college	88.2	17
Art and design college	85.7	7
General further education college	83.1	136
Sixth form college	36.5	63
Specialist designated institution	50.0	4
Tertiary college	68.6	35
Total (N=100%)	**69.8**	**262**

Table A28. Students with learning difficulties and/or disabilities receiving non-FEFC-funded learning support, by FEFC region

FEFC region	Colleges receiving non-FEFC-funded learning support	Respondents
	%	No.
East Midlands	65.0	20
Eastern Region	78.6	28
Greater London	78.8	33
North West	70.6	34
Northern Region	64.3	13
South East	66.7	33
South West	87.5	24
West Midlands	65.9	44
Yorkshire and Humberside	53.1	32
Total (N=100%)	**69.8**	**261**

Table A29. Students with learning difficulties and/or disabilities receiving non-FEFC-funded learning support, by college size

Enrolled students	Colleges receiving non-FEFC-funded learning support	Respondents
	%	No.
0–999	51.2	41
1,000–2,499	47.2	53
2,500–4,999	78.6	42
5,000–7,499	83.6	61
7,500–9,999	92.9	28
10,000 or more	73.0	37
Total (N=100%)	**69.8**	**262**

Note: college size as at November 1994

69

Mapping Provision: The Provision of and Participation in Further Education by Students with Learning Difficulties and/or Disabilities

Appendix 1

Table A30. Non-FEFC sources of additional support funding

Funding source	Colleges with students whose learning support is financed by the source in question	
	No.	*%*
Internal institution budget	108	60.3
LEA	88	49.2
TEC	67	37.4
Social Services	63	35.2
HA	41	22.9
ESF	38	21.2
Other*	38	21.2
Total (N=100%)	**179**	**100.0**

* *'other' includes a range of alternative sources of funding, the most common being charities and voluntary organisations supporting people with disabilities*
Note: figures total to more than 100%, as respondents could indicate more than one funding source; LEA=local education authority; TEC=training and enterprise council; HA=health authority; ESF=European social fund

Table A31. Non-FEFC sources of additional funding, by type of institution

Funding source	Colleges with students whose learning support is funded by the source in question				
	Sixth form	*Tertiary*	*Art & design*	*Gen FE*	*Agric/hort*
	%	*%*	*%*	*%*	*%*
Internal institution budget	73.9	62.5	80.0	58.9	35.7
LEA	39.1	58.3	20.0	54.5	21.4
TEC	8.7	29.2	0.0	42.9	71.4
Social Services	30.4	33.3	0.0	39.3	28.6
HA	4.3	20.8	0.0	29.5	14.3
ESF	17.4	20.8	0.0	24.1	14.3
Other	4.3	37.5	20.0	23.2	7.1
Total (no. of respondents =)	**23**	**24**	**5**	**112**	**14**

Table A32. Non-FEFC sources of additional funding, by college size

Funding source	Colleges in size category with students whose learning support is funded by the source in question					
	0–999	1,000 – 2,499	2,500 – 4,999	5,000 – 7,499	7,500 – 9,999	10,000 or more
	%	%	%	%	%	%
Internal institution budget	42.1	72.0	64.5	52.9	57.7	74.1
LEA	15.8	28.0	61.3	49.0	57.7	70.4
TEC	36.8	12.0	48.4	43.1	38.5	37.0
Social Services	21.1	20.0	38.7	29.4	57.7	44.4
HA	5.3	4.0	16.1	21.6	38.5	48.1
ESF	15.8	16.0	16.1	25.5	23.1	25.9
Other	10.5	24.0	25.8	23.5	19.2	18.5
Total (no. of respondents =) 19		**25**	**31**	**51**	**28**	**37**

Note: LEA=local education authority; TEC=training and enterprise council; HA=health authority; ESF=European social fund; college size as at November 1994

Table A33. Existence of internal unmet need, by type of institution

Institution type	Colleges identifying enrolled students with learning difficulties and/or disabilities whose learning support needs cannot be met in full			
	Yes	No	Don't know	N=
	%	%	%	
Agriculture and horticulture college	27.8	66.7	5.6	18
Art and design college	14.3	71.4	14.3	7
General further education college	34.6	56.6	8.8	136
Sixth form college	23.1	70.8	6.2	65
Specialist designated institution	20.0	60.0	20.0	5
Tertiary college	30.6	63.9	5.6	36
Total (N=100%)	**30.0**	**62.2**	**7.9**	**267**

Table A34. Existence of internal unmet need, by FEFC region

FEFC region	Colleges identifying enrolled students with learning difficulties and/or disabilities whose learning support needs cannot be met in full			
	Yes %	*No* %	*Don't know* %	*N=*
East Midlands	16.7	61.1	22.2	18
Eastern Region	35.7	64.4	0.0	28
Greater London	45.7	48.6	5.7	35
North West	25.7	65.7	8.6	35
Northern Region	13.3	73.3	13.3	15
South East	34.3	51.4	14.3	35
South West	28.0	64.0	8.0	25
West Midlands	23.3	74.4	2.3	43
Yorkshire and Humberside	33.3	60.6	6.1	33
Total (N=100%)	**30.0**	**62.2**	**7.9**	**267**

Table A35. Existence of internal unmet need, by college size

Enrolled students	Colleges identifying enrolled students with learning difficulties and/or disabilities whose learning support needs cannot be met in full			
	Yes %	*No* %	*Don't know* %	*N=*
0–999	21.4	64.3	14.3	42
1,000–2,499	28.6	69.6	1.8	56
2,500–4,999	31.0	61.9	7.1	42
5,000–7,499	30.5	57.6	11.9	59
7,500–9,999	42.9	53.6	3.6	28
10,000 or more	30.0	62.5	7.5	40
Total (N=100%)	**30.0**	**62.2**	**7.9**	**267**

Note: college size as at November 1994

Table A36. Systems for recording external unmet need, by type of institution

Institution type	Colleges identifying enrolled students with learning difficulties and/or disabilities whose learning support needs cannot be met in full			
	Yes %	*No* %	*Don't know* %	*N=*
Agriculture and horticulture college	33.3	50.0	16.7	18
Art and design college	42.9	28.6	28.6	7
General further education college	71.9	23.7	4.3	139
Sixth form college	52.4	39.7	7.9	63
Specialist designated institution	40.0	40.0	20.0	5
Tertiary college	72.2	22.2	5.6	36
Total (N=100%)	**63.4**	**29.5**	**7.1**	**268**

Table A37. Systems for recording external unmet need, by FEFC region

FEFC region	Colleges identifying potential students with learning difficulties and/or disabilities who applied but could not be enrolled			
	Yes	*No*	*Don't know*	*N=*
	%	%	%	
East Midlands	42.1	42.1	15.8	19
Eastern Region	67.9	32.1	0.0	28
Greater London	71.4	22.9	5.7	35
North West	65.7	20.0	14.3	35
Northern Region	92.3	7.7	0.0	13
South East	61.8	26.5	11.8	34
South West	53.8	38.5	7.7	26
West Midlands	66.7	31.1	2.2	45
Yorkshire and Humberside	54.5	39.4	6.1	33
Total (N=100%)	**63.4**	**29.5**	**7.1**	**268**

Table A38. Systems for recording external unmet need, by college size

Enrolled students	Colleges identifying potential students with learning difficulties and/or disabilities who applied but could not be enrolled			
	Yes	*No*	*Don't know*	*N=*
	%	%	%	
0–999	45.2	35.7	19.0	42
1,000–2,499	47.3	47.3	5.5	55
2,500–4,999	64.3	26.2	9.5	42
5,000–7,499	68.9	26.2	4.9	61
7,500–9,999	89.3	10.7	0.0	28
10,000 or more	77.5	20.0	2.5	40
Total (N=100%)	**63.4**	**29.5**	**7.1**	**268**

Note: college size as at November 1994

Table A39. Perceived estimates of extent of external unmet need, by type of institution

Institution type	Potential students with learning difficulties and/or disabilities 'turned away' for each college	N=
	No.	
Agriculture and horticulture college	0.4	5
Art and design college	1.0	3
General further education college	5.5	86
Sixth form college	1.0	31
Specialist designated institution	0.0	2
Tertiary college	3.5	23
Total (N=100%)	**3.9**	**150**

Note: based on average number of potential students

Appendix 1

Table A40. Perceived estimates of extent of external unmet need, by FEFC region

FEFC region	Potential students with learning difficulties and/or disabilities 'turned away' for each college	N=
	No.	
East Midlands	1.1	7
Eastern Region	5.2	17
Greater London	7.3	20
North West	2.3	17
Northern Region	4.8	11
South East	2.6	20
South West	3.9	13
West Midlands	3.6	28
Yorkshire and Humberside	2.8	17
Total (N=100%)	**3.9**	**150**

Note: based on average number of potential students

Table A41. Perceived estimates of extent of external unmet need, by college size

Enrolled students	Potential students with learning difficulties and/or disabilities 'turned away' for each college	N=
	No.	
0–999	0.8	18
1,000–2,499	1.0	24
2,500–4,999	4.8	26
5,000–7,499	4.3	37
7,500–9,999	7.3	21
10,000 or more	4.6	24
Total (N=100%)	**3.9**	**150**

Note: based on average number of potential students; college size as at November 1994

Table A42. Perceptions of other local providers' ability to meet unmet need, by type of institution

Institution type	Colleges aware of unmet need which they believe other local providers can meet			
	Yes %	No %	Don't know %	N=
Agriculture and horticulture college	25.0	25.0	50.0	4
Art and design college	50.0	50.0	0.0	2
General further education college	42.5	42.5	14.9	87
Sixth form college	66.7	0.0	33.3	18
Tertiary college	33.3	42.9	23.8	21
Total (N=100%)	**43.9**	**36.4**	**19.7**	**132**

Table A43. Perceptions of other local providers' ability to meet unmet need, by FEFC

region

FEFC region	Colleges aware of unmet need which they believe other local providers can meet			
	Yes %	No %	Don't know %	N=
East Midlands	28.6	28.6	42.9	7
Eastern Region	33.3	53.3	13.3	15
Greater London	66.7	16.7	16.7	18
North West	52.6	26.3	21.1	19
Northern Region	66.7	0.0	33.3	9
South East	47.1	41.2	11.8	17
South West	41.7	50.0	8.3	12
West Midlands	27.3	54.5	18.2	22
Yorkshire and Humberside	30.8	38.5	30.8	13
Total (N=100%)	**43.9**	**36.4**	**19.7**	**132**

Note: college size as at November 1994

Table A44. Perceptions of other local providers' ability to meet unmet need, by college size

Enrolled students	Colleges aware of unmet need which they believe other local providers can meet			
	Yes %	No %	Don't know %	N=
0–999	36.4	27.3	36.4	11
1,000–2,499	66.7	6.7	26.7	15
2,500–4,999	39.1	34.8	26.1	23
5,000–7,499	35.3	52.9	11.8	34
7,500–9,999	47.6	38.1	14.3	21
10,000 or more	46.4	35.7	17.9	28
Total (N=100%)	**43.9**	**36.4**	**19.7**	**132**

Note: college size as at November 1994

Table A45. Which other local providers could meet unmet need?

Local providers which can meet learning support needs which respondents cannot	Respondents	
	No.	%
Other further education sector institution	20	35.7
Specialist provider	11	19.6
Residential provider	3	5.4
Social services	6	10.7
Charity/voluntary sector provider	2	3.6
Multiple providers	11	19.6
Unknown	3	5.4
Total (N=100%)	**56**	**100.0**

Table A46. Identifying potential but currently unexpressed demand, by type of institution

Institution type	Colleges identifying potential demand for FE among local population with learning difficulties and/or disabilities			
	Yes %	No %	Don't know %	N=
Agriculture and horticulture college	55.6	33.3	11.1	18
Art and design college	83.3	0.0	16.7	6
General further education college	79.6	17.5	2.9	137
Sixth form college	44.4	47.6	7.9	63
Specialist designated institution	0.0	57.1	14.3	5
Tertiary college	84.8	15.2	0.0	33
Total (N=100%)	**66.8**	**28.2**	**5.0**	**262**

Table A47. Identifying potential but currently unexpressed demand, by FEFC region

FEFC region	Colleges identifying potential demand for FE among local population with learning difficulties and/or disabilities			
	Yes %	No %	Don't know %	N=
East Midlands	61.1	27.8	11.1	18
Eastern Region	82.1	17.9	0.0	28
Greater London	64.7	26.5	8.8	34
North West	77.1	17.1	5.7	35
Northern Region	69.2	30.8	0.0	13
South East	62.9	34.3	2.9	35
South West	64.0	32.0	4.0	25
West Midlands	57.1	33.3	9.5	42
Yorkshire and Humberside	65.6	34.4	0.0	32
Total (N=100%)	**66.8**	**28.2**	**5.0**	**262**

Table A48. Identifying potential but currently unexpressed demand, by college size

Enrolled students	Colleges identifying potential demand for FE among local population with learning difficulties and/or disabilities			
	Yes %	No %	Don't know %	N=
0–999	31.7	51.2	17.1	41
1,000–2,499	50.9	45.3	3.8	53
2,500–4,999	79.1	16.3	4.7	43
5,000–7,499	73.3	25.0	1.7	60
7,500–9,999	96.2	3.8	0.0	26
10,000 or more	82.1	15.4	2.6	39
Total (N=100%)	**66.8**	**28.2**	**5.0**	**262**

Note: college size as at November 1994

Table A49. Overall approach to provision for students with learning difficulties and/or disabilities, by type of institution

Statement	Average score for each statement (1='strongly agree' ...... 5='strongly disagree')					
	Sixth form	Tertiary	Art & design	Gen FE	Agric/hort	Specialist
There is a cross-institution approach to learning support	1.9	1.4	1.6	1.6	1.6	2.6
The institution has a policy of 'open access' to all potential students irrespective of learning difficulty and/or disability	2.3	1.6	1.3	1.7	2.3	2.6
The institution employs specialist learning support staff who meet most learning support needs	2.4	1.7	1.7	1.7	1.7	3.4
All students are assessed for learning support needs	2.8	2.4	1.9	2.6	1.8	2.3
Learning support is mostly provided by lecturing/tutorial staff	2.4	2.6	3.1	2.6	3.1	2.0
The main provision for students with learning difficulties and/or disabilities is on 'discrete' courses	4.4	3.7	3.6	3.1	3.4	3.7
Students are assessed for learning support only if self-identified, or on the basis of prior information	3.6	4.2	3.4	3.7	4.4	3.7

Appendix 1

Table A50. Overall approach to provision for students with learning difficulties and/or disabilities, by college size

Statement	*Average score for each statement (1='strongly agree' ...... 5='strongly disagree')*					
	0–999	*1,000– 2,499*	*2,500– 4,999*	*5,000– 7,499*	*7,500– 9,999*	*10,000 or more*
There is a cross-institution approach to learning support	1.9	1.8	1.7	1.4	1.6	1.7
The institution has a policy of 'open access' to all potential students irrespective of learning difficulty and/or disability	2.5	2.0	1.9	1.6	1.7	1.6
The institution employs specialist learning support staff who meet most learning support needs	2.5	2.0	1.9	1.7	1.7	1.7
All students are assessed for learning support needs	2.4	2.4	2.5	2.5	2.9	2.7
Learning support is mostly provided by lecturing/tutorial staff	2.6	2.5	2.8	2.4	2.5	2.7
The main provision for students with learning difficulties and/or disabilities is on 'discrete' courses	4.1	4.1	2.9	3.4	3.2	3.2
Students are assessed for learning support only if self-identified, or on the basis of prior information	3.8	3.8	3.7	4.0	3.8	3.5

Note: college size as at November 1994

Questionnaire

Mapping Provision and Participation in Further Education by People with Learning Difficulties and/or Disabilities

Please answer the following questions as fully as you are able by ticking the boxes or writing in the spaces provided. Please return the completed questionnaire to IES in the reply-paid envelope provided. If you have any queries, please contact Nigel Meager or Sally Dench at IES: telephone 01273 686751.

Please return by 1 January 1996, or sooner if possible. Thank you for your co-operation.

Purpose

This questionnaire aims to collect data about the provision for and participation of students with learning difficulties and/or disabilities in further education in England.

The questionnaire has been commissioned by the learning difficulties and/or disabilities committee. For its final report, to be published next year, the committee wants to have comprehensive data to enable it to:

- report on how many students with learning difficulties and/or disabilities are studying in further education;

- consider how far the provision and support available to them meets their needs;

- consider how the Council can most usefully collect relevant data in future to enable it and colleges to monitor provision and participation;

- offer advice to colleges which will help them better to identify demand in their locality from these learners.

Scope

The questionnaire has been designed following a pilot exercise with colleges during the summer and with advice from an advisory group. The scope of the questionnaire has been simplified considerably and more detailed guidance on its completion prepared, in the light of that pilot. We are grateful to those colleges which have already helped to shape the questionnaire in this way.

Our aim is to collect as much data as possible on each question from each college, based on the data which they already hold. The questionnaire is not intended to require colleges to collect new data or to collect data in new ways. **Thus, if there is anything which the college cannot provide from its existing records without placing excessive demands upon staff, please indicate this on the questionnaire, together with the reason why.**

Rationale

The committee is aware that each college is required to complete the individualised student record (ISR) return with a reference date of 1 November 1995. This questionnaire is designed to complement but not to duplicate that data return. The questionnaire does not ask colleges for any basic data that can be obtained from the ISR data returns.

However, the committee does need some information not collected in the ISR if it is to be in a position to fulfil its remit. Specifically, the ISR records students who assess themselves as disabled and those for whom the college is providing additional support. Whilst essential data, neither of these two ISR categories is designed to count all and only those students with a learning difficulty and/or disability. The ISR data will not, for example:

- identify students with a learning difficulty who do not assess themselves as having a disability;

Appendix 2

- identify students who are receiving additional support because of a learning difficulty and/or disability and not for another reason (for example, basic skill needs);

- identify any characteristics of students receiving additional support or the nature of the additional support they are receiving.

The relationship between the data collected by the ISR and those sought by this questionnaire is shown in the diagram below.

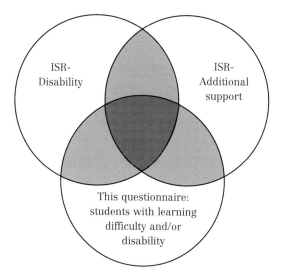

Terminology

The following terminology is used throughout the questionnaire:

Students with learning difficulties and/or disabilities — as defined in section 4 of the *Further and Higher Education Act 1992*, that is, students who have a significantly greater difficulty in learning than the majority of their peers. This excludes students who need extra help with their literacy, numeracy or the English language for reasons other than their learning difficulty and/or disability.

Learning support — learning support given to students beyond that usually available through the delivery of the student's main programme of study. Learning support may or may not be of a kind and cost covered by additional support (see below). Learning support does not include support for learners because of their personal circumstances (for example, a crèche) but may include elements

of support ineligible for funding under the additional support bands, such as personal equipment.

Additional support — learning support given to students beyond that usually available through the delivery of the student's main programme of study, where this is funded by the additional support bands within the Council's recurrent funding methodology. The number of students receiving additional support are, therefore, those receiving learning support funded via this mechanism. The number will, therefore, be smaller than those receiving learning support, because learning support includes a wider range of activities and costs than are included in the additional support mechanism.

Full time — at least 450 guided learning hours.

Part time — less than 450 guided learning hours.

Structure

The questionnaire is structured as follows:

Section 1 asks about the systems in place within the college to identify students enrolling at the college who have a learning difficulty and/or disability; and asks for some data about the number of students with a learning difficulty and/or disability who are enrolled;

Section 2 asks about the characteristics of students with learning difficulties and/or disabilities and their learning support needs. It also seeks information on the provision of support to students who have additional needs for reasons not related to a learning difficulty and/or disability;

Section 3 asks about the costs of providing learning support to students with learning difficulties and/or disabilities, and sources of funding;

Section 4 asks about unmet needs; and

Finally, Section 5 asks about the institution's overall approach to provision for students with learning difficulties and/or disabilities.

80

Mapping Provision: The Provision of and Participation in Further Education by Students with Learning Difficulties and/or Disabilities

Completing the questionnaire

It is likely that much of the information will be held by the college learning support team or co-ordinator, although we hope that the MIS manager will also be closely involved.

The college principal is asked to sign off the completed return so that we can be confident it represents the college's formal response and that the data match as far as possible with the college's ISR return.

Colleges are asked to send completed questionnaires to:

> **The Institute for Employment Studies, Mantell Building, University of Sussex, Falmer, Brighton BN1 9RF, by 1st January 1996.**

Status of the data

The data are being collected on behalf of the learning difficulties and/or disabilities committee. However, given the intention that this questionnaire should not duplicate the data available from the ISR, the objective of presenting a full picture of participation and provision can be achieved only if the data from this questionnaire are put alongside that from the college's ISR return.

The use of the data will be governed by the principles set out in the ISR college support manual.

81

Mapping Provision: The Provision of and Participation in Further Education by Students with Learning Difficulties and/or Disabilities

Appendix 2

MAPPING PROVISION AND PARTICIPATION IN FURTHER EDUCATION BY PEOPLE WITH LEARNING DIFFICULTIES AND/OR DISABILITIES

College name:

FEFC code:

1. **STUDENTS WITH LEARNING DIFFICULTIES AND/OR DISABILITIES**

1.1 How does this institution attempt formally to **identify** enrolled students **who have a learning difficulty and/or disability?** (*please tick*)

	Full-time	*Part-time*
a) college attempts to identify **all** students with learning difficulties and/or disabilities irrespective of whether they need learning support	❑	❑
b) students with learning difficulties and/or disabilities are identified only through self-identification	❑	❑
c) students with learning difficulties and/or disabilities are identified only where there is a learning support need	❑	❑

1.2 Please complete the boxes below, indicating the number of students enrolled at this institution (at 1 November 1995) who have been identified as having a **learning difficulty and/or disability**, whether or not they have been identified as needing any learning support or additional support.

	Males	*Females*	*Total*
Part-time students	☐	☐	☐
Full-time students	☐	☐	☐
All students identified as having a learning difficulty and/or disability			☐

1.3 Please indicate the numbers of full- and part-time students with a learning difficulty and/or disability, by age group. *(Age is defined as at 31 August 1995).*

	16 to 18	19 to 24	25 and over
Part-time students	☐	☐	☐
Full-time students	☐	☐	☐

(note: numbers should sum to the total given in Q1.2 above)

1.4 Please indicate the number of students with a learning difficulty and/or disability, by ethnic group

White	Black-Caribbean	Black-African	Black-other
☐	☐	☐	☐

Indian	Pakistani	Bangladeshi	Chinese
☐	☐	☐	☐

Other Asian	Other	Ethnic group unknown
☐	☐	☐

(note: numbers should sum to the total given in Q1.2 above)

1.5 How many students with a learning difficulty and/or disability
   (as at 1 November 1995) are following a programme:

	Full-time	Part-time	Total
a) designed for any student			
b) designed solely or primarily for students with learning difficulties and/or disabilities			
c) combining elements of (a) and (b) above			

(note: numbers should sum to the total given in Q1.2 above)

1.6 How many students with a learning difficulty and/or disability are studying at each of the following levels?

Pre-vocational/foundation ☐

(G)NVQ Level 1 or equivalent ☐

(G)NVQ Level 2 or equivalent — including GCSEs ☐

(G)NVQ Level 3 or equivalent — including GCE A/AS level ☐

(G)NVQ Level 4 or equivalent ☐

(note: numbers should sum to the total given in Q1.2 above)

1.7 Are there, to your knowledge, students enrolled in this institution who have a learning difficulty and/or disability, but who have not been formally identified as such? *(please tick one box)*

Yes ☐ 1   No ☐ 2   Don't know ☐ 3
                go to section 2   *go to section 2*

1.8 If YES, is it possible to make a broad estimate of the number of such students? *(please tick one box)*

Yes ☐ 1   No ☐ 2   Don't know ☐ 3
                go to section 2   *go to section 2*

1.9 If YES, please indicate your estimate in the boxes below, distinguishing if possible between full- and part-time students:

Total ☐

Full-time ☐

Part-time ☐

2. CHARACTERISTICS OF AND LEARNING SUPPORT FOR STUDENTS WITH LEARNING DIFFICULTIES AND/OR DISABILITIES (AS AT 1 NOVEMBER 1995)

2.1 Please enter the following information in the table below.

For each characteristic of learning difficulty and/or disability, please indicate:

a)   the total number of enrolled students with the characteristic in question;

b)   the total number with the characteristic receiving learning support;

c)   of (b), the number whose learning support is funded under the FEFC additional support bands;

d)   and of (b), the number whose learning support is funded from non-FEFC sources

(note (c) and (d) may not sum to (b) if some students are funded from both sources.)

	(a) total	(b) number receiving learning support	(c) of (b): no. funded through FEFC additional support bands	(d) of (b): no. with some or all learning support funded from non-FEFC sources
1. Characteristics of learning difficulty and/or disability				
Visual impairment				
Hearing impairment				
Disability affecting mobility				
Other physical disability				
Other medical condition (eg, epilepsy, asthma, diabetes)				
Moderate learning difficulties				
Severe learning difficulties				
Specific learning difficulties (eg, dyslexia, dyscalcula)				
Emotional/behavioural difficulties				
Mental ill health				
Temporary disability after illness (eg, post-viral) or accident				
Profound/complex disabilities				
Multiple disabilities*				
Other (*please specify*):				
Totals =				

Notes: Please include all those with multiple disabilities in the category labelled 'multiple disabilities' rather than under each individual characteristic.*
The total in column (a) should be the same as that given in Q1.2. above.

2.2 For all students with learning difficulties and/or disabilities:.

(a) Please indicate the number of students with learning difficulties and/or disabilities who receive each of the types of learning support listed below. We are interested in all learning support, not just additional support. Please add anything which is not included in the list, and the number of students involved. Please include types of provision you buy in as well as those provided by the college directly.

(b) Tick the following box if this support is wholly or partly funded via the FEFC additional support mechanism.

Nature of facility/ support provision:	(a) No. of students in receipt of learning support (or tick if number not available)	(b) support wholly or partly funded through FEFC additional support bands
Support assistants (non-teaching)		
Class support from additional teacher		
Supplementary teaching (outside main course)		
Communicators and specialist teaching (for students who are deaf or hard of hearing)		
Taping/Brailling		
Specialist teaching/support for blind/partially-sighted people		
Specialist equipment		
Physiotherapy		
Speech/communication/language therapy		
Nursing support/medical services		
Specialist counselling for disabled people		
Specialist psychiatric support		
Social work support		
Specialist careers advice		
Educational psychology		
Specialist assessment		
Drop-in support centres (eg, basic skills workshops)		
Transport between sites		
Transport between home and college		
Cross-college learning support team(s)		
Other *(specify)*		
Other *(specify)*		

85

Mapping Provision: The Provision of and Participation in Further Education by Students with Learning Difficulties and/or Disabilities

2.3 How many students receive additional support funded by FEFC for reasons other than a learning difficulty and/or disability, for example, students with basic skills problems (ie literacy, numeracy) not related to a learning difficulty and/or disability; and ESOL students?

Number funded through FEFC additional support bands [ ]

Note: This figure, when added to the total in column (c) of Q 2.1, should equate to the number of students receiving additional support recorded in the institution's ISR return.

3. **THE COST OF AND FUNDING FOR LEARNING SUPPORT AS AT 1 NOVEMBER 1995**

In this section we are concerned only with the **provision of learning support for students with learning difficulties and/or disabilities**, ie, do not include students who have other learning support needs (eg, basic skills, ESOL), but who do not also have a learning difficulty and/or disability.

3.1 Please indicate the number of students whose additional support is funded by the FEFC.

Annual cost per student:

£170–500 [ ]	£501–£1,000 [ ]
£1,001–£2,000 [ ]	£2,001–£4,000 [ ]
£4,001–£5,600 [ ]	£5,601–£8,800 [ ]
over £8,800 [ ]	Total [ ]

3.2 Are there students with learning difficulties and/or disabilities receiving learning support which is (wholly or partly) funded by non-FEFC sources?

Yes ☐   No ☐

If YES, please indicate which sources are used, by writing 1 in the box referring to the most important etc. (if the source is not used, leave the box blank).

LEA [ ]   TEC [ ]   ESF [ ]   Soc.services [ ]

Health Auth. [ ]   Internal college budget [ ]   Other *(please specify)* [ ]

4. **UNMET NEED**

This section is concerned with the **institution's ability to meet** the learning support needs of students and potential students with learning difficulties and/or disabilities.

Internal unmet need

By 'internal unmet need', we mean the learning support needs of **already enrolled students with learning difficulties and/or disabilities**, which the college is unable to meet, or unable to meet in full.

4.1 Are there any enrolled students who have been **identified** as having learning support needs, whose needs the institution is not able to meet or meet in full, excluding students who decide not to take up the support offered.

Yes [ ] 1   No [ ] 2   Don't know [ ] 3

go to question 4.5   go to question 4.5

86

Mapping Provision: The Provision of and Participation in Further Education by Students with Learning Difficulties and/or Disabilities

If YES,

4.2   Please indicate if possible, the number of such students

[   ]

4.3   Please list the nature of the needs involved:

4.4   Why is it not possible to meet these needs?

External unmet need

By 'external unmet need', we mean the learning support needs of **potential students with learning difficulties and/or disabilities, who are unable to participate in further education at this college**, because the institution is unable to meet these needs.

For those who applied to enrol at the college for 1995/96:

4.5   Does the college have systems in place to record cases where potential students with a learning difficulty and/or disability apply to the college, but cannot be enrolled for any reason?

Yes [   ] 1   No [   ] 2   Don't know [   ] 3

go to question 4.9   *go to question 4.9*

If YES,

4.6   Please indicate the number of such students during the 1995/6 academic year.

[   ]

4.7   Please list the nature of the learning support needs involved, and say briefly why it was not possible to meet these needs.

4.8   Do you know whether other local providers meet these needs?

Yes [   ] 1   No [   ] 2   Don't know [   ] 3

If YES, please indicate **which** providers, and which needs they are able to meet:

For those who have yet to, or do not usually apply to enrol at the college:

4.9   Does the college have any way of identifying the potential, **currently unexpressed demand** for participation in further education among people with learning difficulties and/or disabilities within the local population?

Yes [   ] 1   No [   ] 2   Don't know [   ] 3

go to section 5   *go to section 5*

87

Mapping Provision: The Provision of and Participation in Further Education by Students with Learning Difficulties and/or Disabilities

4.10 If YES, please indicate, if possible, your estimate of the number of such potential students per year with learning difficulties and/or disabilities in your catchment area [ ] and please indicate which information sources are used to contribute to identifying unexpressed demand for participants in FE: *(please tick all those which apply)*

- ❏ Formal links with schools
- ❏ Social/health services
- ❏ Local/regional statistics (eg, census and other demographic information)
- ❏ Community outreach work
- ❏ Careers Service
- ❏ Voluntary organisation
- ❏ College needs analysis/marketing
- ❏ Informal contacts
- ❏ Own survey/research
- ❏ Other *(please specify)*

5. OVERALL APPROACH TO PROVISION FOR STUDENTS WITH LEARNING DIFFICULTIES AND/OR DISABILITIES

5.1 How would you describe your institution's overall approach to provision for students with learning difficulties and/or disabilities? Please indicate how far you agree with each of the following statements as a description of this institution's overall approach to provision for students with learning difficulties and/or disabilities?

	1 strongly agree	2 agree	3 neither agree nor disagree	4 disagree	5 strongly disagree
The institution has a policy of 'open access' to all potential students irrespective of learning difficulty and/or disability.	❏	❏	❏	❏	❏
There is a cross-college approach to learning support	❏	❏	❏	❏	❏
The institution employs specialist learning support staff who meet most learning support needs	❏	❏	❏	❏	❏
Learning support is mostly provided by lecturing/tutorial staff	❏	❏	❏	❏	❏
All students are assessed for learning support needs	❏	❏	❏	❏	❏
Students are assessed for learning support only if self-identified, or on the basis of prior information	❏	❏	❏	❏	❏
The main provision for students with learning difficulties and/or disabilities is on 'discrete' courses	❏	❏	❏	❏	❏

Mapping Provision: The Provision of and Participation in Further Education by Students with Learning Difficulties and/or Disabilities

If you wish to add any further information about your institution's approach to, or provision for, students with learning difficulties and/or disabilities; its approach to assessment and learning support; or the main changes in the provision made by your institution since incorporation, please use the space below, or continue on a separate sheet.

Signed: Date:
(College Principal)

Thank you for completing the questionnaire.

Please return to the Institute for Employment Studies, Mantell Building, University of Sussex, Falmer, Brighton BN1 9RF using the reply-paid envelope provided.

Tel: 01273 686751 Fax: 01273 690430.

89

Mapping Provision: The Provision of and Participation in Further Education by Students with Learning Difficulties and/or Disabilities

Summary of the Work to Estimate the Incidence of Learning Difficulties and/or Disabilities in the Population

Introduction

The results of research to estimate the number of people aged 16 and over in England with learning difficulties and/or disabilities are summarised below. The aim of this part of the project was to estimate, from existing data, the number of people aged 16 and over in each region in England with learning difficulties and/or disabilities. If successful, this would enable participation rates in further education for people with learning difficulties and/or disabilities to be calculated.

Background

There are two sources of information about the population with a learning difficulty and/or disability:

- administrative records;
- population survey data.

Administrative sources record the number of people presenting themselves for services, for example for benefits, and cannot generally be used to estimate prevalence. Population survey data record all people with a particular characteristic either from the population as a whole or for a sample of the population, not just those using services.

Relevant data sets and previous research were examined to determine to what extent the available statistics could provide reliable estimates of the number of people aged 16 and over with learning difficulties and/or disabilities in England.

Defining learning difficulty and/or disability

No common definition of learning difficulty and/or disability exists. A review of the evidence in this area confirmed that:

- there is a number of different definitions of learning difficulty and/or disability in legislation;
- there is no common definition of learning difficulty and/or disability among practitioners;
- the definition and terminology used to describe learning difficulties and/or disabilities can be different in education than in other sectors;
- there are differences in the definitions and terminology used to describe learning difficulties and/or disabilities within the education sector.

The *Further and Higher Education Act 1992* (the Act) provides the legal framework within which the Further Education Funding Council (the Council) operates. The Act states that 'a person has a learning difficulty if:

- he has significantly greater difficulty in learning than the majority of persons of his age, or
- he has a disability which prevents or hinders him from making use of facilities of a kind generally provided by institutions within the further education sector for persons of his age.'

The Act also states that 'a person should not be taken to have a learning difficulty solely because the language, or form of language, in which he will be taught is different from that which has at any time been spoken in his home.'

No definition is offered of the phrases 'generally provided' or 'significantly greater difficulty'. In the Act, the phrase 'learning difficulty' is used to include both those with a difficulty in learning of any kind and those whose disability prevents them participating in the kind of further education enjoyed by their peers.

91

Mapping Provision: The Provision of and Participation in Further Education by Students with Learning Difficulties and/or Disabilities

Target population

The target population of those with learning difficulties and/or disabilities for the purposes of this project was determined, after discussion with the advisory group for the project, as:

• people with cognitive difficulties in medical terms; other terms used historically or by the medical profession are mental handicap, mental retardation or intellectual disability; within the education sector the term 'learning difficulty' is commonly used to describe this group; within the health and social services sectors the term 'learning disability' is commonly used;

• people with a specific learning difficulty such as dyslexia or dyscalcula;

• people with sensory or physical disabilities or impairments who do not necessarily have a difficulty with learning but who may have additional support requirements in order to participate in further education;

• people with mental ill health problems;

• people with emotional or behavioural difficulties with additional support requirements; and

• people who have more than one or more of the above characteristics, on a temporary or permanent basis.

The focus of the project is primarily people of working age. The target group includes people who are improving their basic literacy or numeracy skills who have a learning difficulty or disability, but does not encompass all those learners who are improving their basic literacy or numeracy

skills. People for whom English is not their first language who are experiencing learning difficulties for this reason alone are also not included in the scope of the project.

Results

Existing data sources do not allow a reliable estimate of the population with learning difficulties and/or disabilities of England to be calculated. There is a paucity of data in the area of learning difficulties in particular and the information which is available can be inconsistent. A number of sources give partial information for subsets of the target population. These are described further below. Fuller details of the data sources investigated are available from IES on request.

People with disabilities

There were an estimated 1.8 million people aged between 16 and 59 in England in 1995 with a disability and an additional 4 million people aged 60 and over with a disability (see table 1). The number of people with disabilities increases markedly with age. Sixty per cent of people living in private households who have a disability are aged 60 or over. In communal establishments, 88% of people who have disabilities are 60 years of age and over.

The estimates are calculated using prevalence rates from surveys of disability undertaken by the Office of Population Censuses and Surveys (OPCS) in the period 1985 to 1988, applied to mid-1995 population estimates. The calculation

Table 1. Estimated number of adults with a disability in England, 1995

Population (000s)	Age group						
	16–19	20–29	30–39	40–49	50–59	16–59	60+
In private households	45	207	312	453	689	1,706	3,555
In communal establishments	1	16	17	9	11	53	403
Total	46	223	329	462	700	1,759	3,958

Source: OPCS Surveys of Disabilities in Great Britain Report 1; OPCS mid-1995 population projections

92

Mapping Provision: The Provision of and Participation in Further Education by Students with Learning Difficulties and/or Disabilities

assumes that the prevalence rates found in the 1985 survey are broadly the same in 1995. The OPCS surveys allow national estimates of disability to be calculated, but regional and sub-regional estimates which are disaggregated by age group or other characteristics are prone to sampling errors.

Compared with the target population for this study, the OPCS surveys are likely to exclude people with moderate learning difficulties, people with a specific learning difficulty such as dyslexia, some people with mental ill health problems or with emotional or behavioural difficulties. In addition, the OPCS surveys did not include coverage of educational establishments, places of detention or military establishments. In consequence, the number of 16 to 19 year olds with a disability living in communal establishments will be an underestimate.

People with disabilities: comparisons between sources of data

Table 2 shows a broad comparison between the updated OPCS estimates and the following other sources:

- the 1992 General Household Survey (GHS);
- the 1991 Census of Population;
- the winter 1993 Labour Force Survey (LFS);
- Department of Health administrative registers which include a register of general classes of disability, persons registered as blind or partially-sighted and persons registered as deaf or hard of hearing.

The GHS and the LFS are sample surveys. The 1991 Census of Population covers the resident population of Great Britain.

The comparison shows that for adults of working age living in private households:

- estimates of the number of people with a disability vary enormously between the five sources. The different years to which the data relate do not account for the differences which are due to definitional variations;
- the estimates from the GHS of the number of people with a disability are much higher than the estimates from other sources, at almost 6 million in 1992. This is likely to be due to the phrasing of the question in the GHS which relates to any long-standing illness, disability or infirmity which limits the activities of the respondent;
- the LFS gives a much lower estimate of 3.1 million people with a disability in 1993. The LFS question asks about any health problems or disabilities which affect the kind of paid work the person can do;
- the estimates from the 1991 Census are of a similar order of magnitude to the updated OPCS survey estimates, with an estimated 1.7 million people with disabilities in 1991. The 1991 Census question asked about any long-term illness, health problem or handicap which limits the daily activities or work the respondent can do;
- the Department of Health records, which are of people registering, are much lower than the other sources which are population estimates.

The 1991 Census records just under 3,000 16 to 19 year olds with a limiting long-term illness living in communal establishments and a further 69,000 living in private households. This is considerably higher than the estimated 46,000 16 to 19 year olds with a disability estimated from the OPCS disability surveys.

For adults over working age there is much more similarity between the sources.

Table 2. Comparison of estimates of people with disabilities: England

Source/year	Persons (000s)	
	Private households	Total
OPCS Surveys of Disability (1995)		
16–59 year olds	1,706	1,759
60 and above	3,555	3,958
Total	5,261	5,717
General Household Survey (1992; GB)		
16–64 year olds	5,917	
65 and above	3,959	
Total	9,876	
1991 Census: Limiting Long-term Illness		
16–59 year olds	1,959	2,036
60 and above	3,407	3,770
Total	5,366	5,806
Labour Force Survey (1993)		
16–59/64	3,140	
Department of Health Registers (1990-1992)		
16–64	n/a	481

Table 3. Numbers of 16–59 year olds with a visual impairment

Updated OPCS survey (1995)	263,000
RNIB survey (1991)	80,000
Department of Health register (age 16–64; 1991)	44,000

Disability by type

The OPCS surveys also allow the estimation of the number of people with certain types of disability. These are compared in table 3 with information from other sources such as the Royal National Institute for the Blind (RNIB) and the Royal National Institute for Deaf People (RNID). In each case there are differences between the estimates from different sources because of definitional differences.

Visual impairment

The updated OPCS surveys give an estimate of 263,000 adults of working age with a visual impairment in 1995. This is much higher than the RNIB estimate of 80,000 in 1991.

The RNIB figures include only those people who would be able to register as blind or partially-sighted and do not include people with mild or moderate sight loss who were included in the OPCS surveys of disability.

The OPCS surveys include a measure of the severity of visual impairment, but this is on a different basis to the RNIB measures making comparison by severity of impairment difficult.

Administrative data from the Department of Health show that in 1991, only 44,000 people aged 16 to 64 were registered as blind or partially sighted, a much lower number than either of the population estimates.

Hearing impairment

In the case of hearing impairment (table 4), the RNID estimate that there were 677,000 adults aged 16 to 59 with a hearing loss greater than 35 decibels (db) in 1995, while the updated OPCS estimate is somewhat lower.

The OPCS surveys considered people's aided hearing ability whereas the RNID estimates are based on people's unaided hearing function. Those with a hearing loss of between 35dB and 45dB often need little more than a hearing aid. The aided hearing function of these individuals would be such that they would not be considered as having a disability in the OPCS surveys of disability. This is likely to account for the smaller numbers recorded in the OPCS survey.

Administrative data from the Department of Health shows that in 1992, only 40,000 people aged 16 to 64 were registered as deaf or hard of hearing, a much lower number than either of the population estimates.

Learning difficulty and/or disability

The Mental Health Foundation estimate that 2% of the UK population have learning disabilities, the majority of which are mild and that four in 1,000 people (0.4% of the population) have moderate, severe or profound learning disabilities (table 5).

Table 4. Numbers of 16–59 year olds with a hearing impairment

Updated OPCS survey (1995)	513,000
RNID (1995)	677,000
Department of Health register (16–64; 1992)	40,000

Table 5. Number of 16–59 year olds with a learning difficulty and/or disability

Updated OPCS survey (1995)	506,000
Mental Health Foundation (1995):	
All levels of learning disability	575,000
Moderate, severe or profound learning disability	115,000

Table 6. Numbers of 16–59 year olds with a learning disability and/or intellectual impairment

Updated OPCS survey (1995)	506,000
Mental Health Foundation (1995):	
All levels of learning disability	575,000
Moderate,severe or profound learning disability	115,000

95

Appendix 3

At an overall level, this is reasonably comparable with the results of the OPCS surveys which give an estimate of 2% of adults aged 16 to 59 living in private households with an 'intellectual functioning' disability. A person was considered to have an intellectual functioning disability in the surveys if, for example, they could not read a short article in a newspaper, could not write a short letter to someone without help and/or could not count well enough to handle money. The OPCS surveys include a measure of the severity of intellectual functioning disability, but this is not easily translatable into the categories mild, moderate, severe or profound used by the Mental Health Foundation.

Mental illness

People with mental illness are part of the target population for the project. The prevalence rate of mental disorders including schizophrenia, affective psychosis, depressive disorders, and anxiety states is estimated (by the Department of Health) to be between 5.3% and 14% of the population. It is likely that only those people with more severe mental illnesses are included in the OPCS surveys of disability.

Conclusions

The conclusion of the advisory group for the project is that it would be misleading to compare the information on the number of students participating in further education with the limited population data described above because:

- there is no one source or combination of sources which can provide a robust estimate of the population with learning difficulties and/or disabilities;

- combining information from a number of different administrative or population survey sources to create an estimate of the population with learning difficulties and/or disabilities would require assumptions to be made about the overlap between sources and would

potentially over or under count particular groups; and

- the information on the number of students participating in further education and the population estimates have been collected on a different definitional basis, making any comparison between them subject to error.

Summary of Findings from the Survey of External Institutions

As explained in chapter 1, in addition to the main survey of all sector colleges, a smaller survey exercise was conducted among a sample of 50 'external institutions' (that is, other institutions providing further education, and in receipt of funding from the FEFC). The sample was randomly chosen from those external institutions in receipt of funding under the FEFC's additional support bands (that is, the sample was representative of this latter group, but not of all external institutions). Responses were received from 31 of these institutions, and although the sample was both too small, and not sufficiently comparable to the sector college sample, for the data to be incorporated in the survey findings presented in the main body of the report, some data from the external institutions survey are presented briefly in this appendix, for information.

The survey questionnaire used was, in all essential respects, identical to that employed in the main college survey (see appendix 2), and the tables presented below can, therefore, be interpreted in the same fashion as their counterparts in the main body of the

report, and in appendix 1. The main *caveat* is that the numbers of cases involved are generally too small to be grossed up to draw conclusions about the external institution population as a whole. Similarly, because of small numbers, the data cannot be broken down in as detailed a fashion as those for the main survey — the tables presented here for external institutions, therefore, cover only a sub-set of the issues addressed in the main college survey.

It should also be noted that some of the basic information available from the individualised student record (ISR) for the sector colleges (notably overall size of the enrolled student population) was not available in comparable form for the external institutions, and the analysis possible is correspondingly limited by this fact.

Table 1 shows the regional distribution of responding external institutions.

Information on the total numbers of students with learning difficulties and/or disabilities was provided by some 30 of the 31 responding external institutions. These institutions identified between them some 7,079 enrolled students with learning difficulties and/or disabilities, an average of 236 for each institution, although this average reflected a very wide range (the

Table 1. External institutions: respondents by FEFC region

FEFC region	Respondents	
	No.	%
East Midlands	3	10
Eastern Region	7	23
Greater London	4	13
North West	3	10
Northern Region	3	10
South East	1	3
South West	6	19
West Midlands	3	10
Yorkshire and Humberside	1	3
Total (N=100%)	31	100.0

97

Mapping Provision: The Provision of and Participation in Further Education by Students with Learning Difficulties and/or Disabilities

number of students with learning difficulties and/or disabilities at any one college varied between 1 and 2,579).

Almost all of these students were part time (99%), and slightly more than half (55%) were female.

The students with learning difficulties and/or disabilities enrolled in external institutions differed from their counterparts in sector colleges not only in terms of the high incidence of part-timers, but also in the large concentration of adult students in this group.

Some 86% were 25 years or older, 13% were 19–24 year olds, and only 1% were in the 16–18 age range.

These personal characteristics, together with the ethnic origin of these students are summarised in table 2.

Table 3 shows that to a greater extent than in the sector as a whole, provision for students with learning difficulties and/or disabilities in these 30 external institutions is predominantly 'discrete' in nature.

Table 2. External institutions: characteristics of students with learning difficulties and/or disabilities

Characteristic	*Students*	*Colleges on which estimate is based*
	%	No.
Sex		29
Male	45	
Female	55	
Mode of attendance		29
Full-time students	1	
Part-time students	99	
Age		30
Under 16	0	
16–18	1	
19–24	13	
25 and older	86	
Ethnic origin		30
White	79	
Black-Caribbean	2	
Black-African	*	
Black-other	*	
Indian	1	
Pakistani	1	
Bangladeshi	*	
Chinese	*	
Other Asian	*	
Other	1	
Ethnic group unknown	15	
All students	**100.0**	**31**

* less than 0.5%

Table 3. External institutions: type of learning programme being followed

Programme type	Students with learning difficulties and/or disabilities following programmes of type				
	Full-time	*Part-time*	*All students*		*part-time students*
			No.	*%*	*%*
a) Programme designed for any student	0	1,761	1,761	25	100
b) Programme designed solely or primarily for students with learning difficulties and/or disabilities	42	5,085	5,127	72	99
c) Programme combining elements of a) and b) above	0	191	191	3	100
Total (N=100%)	**42**	**7,037**	**7,079**	**100**	**99**

Note: based on 30 colleges

Table 4. External institutions: level of learning programme being followed

Level of programme	Students with learning difficulties and/or disabilities following programme level	
	No.	*%*
Pre-vocational/foundation	4,267	66
(G)NVQ Level 1 or equivalent	611	10
(G)NVQ Level 2 or equivalent — including GCSEs	246	4
(G)NVQ Level 3 or equivalent — including GCE A/AS level	58	1
(G)NVQ Level 4 or equivalent	1,231	19
Total (N=100%)	**6,413**	**100**

Note: based on 30 colleges

As with sector colleges, table 4 shows that students with learning difficulties and/or disabilities were for the most part following lower level courses in external institutions (the 19% recorded as following level 4 courses, all related to one institution specialising in courses at this level).

In table 5 we look at the incidence of different types of learning difficulty and/or disability in the external institutions responding to the survey. It can be seen that the distribution of disability types and the extent to which students with different types

of learning difficulty and/or disability receive learning support, differ somewhat from the corresponding patterns observed among sector colleges (table 12 chapter 3). Given the small number of respondents, and the fact that the data for some categories are heavily influenced by the figures for one large institution, extreme caution should be exercised in drawing any conclusions from the patterns observed.

It can be seen, nevertheless, that taking the data for all disability types together, that the proportion of students receiving learning support, and the proportion for whom that support is funded through the FEFC additional support bands are considerably lower than the corresponding proportions for sector colleges shown in table 12.

Table 5 shows students in external institutions funded through the additional support bands (for those 26 institutions providing data), and shows that (in comparison with sector colleges) those receiving funding through the additional support bands are overwhelmingly concentrated in the lower two bands.

In the light of these results it is clearly of interest to examine the (non-FEFC) sources of funding for these students in external institutions and table 7 does this.

In comparison with sector colleges (figure 6 in chapter 4; table A30 in appendix 1) the non-FEFC sources used by respondent external institutions to fund additional learning support are broadly similar, the main difference being the greater reliance on LEA funding, and the lesser reliance on the institutions' internal budgets.

Table 5. External institutions: incidence of different types of learning difficulty and/or disability among enrolled students, and learning support received

Characteristics of learning difficulty and/or disability	Enrolled students with characteristic		Those receiving learning support*	Those receiving support funded through FEFC additional support bands
	No.	%	%	%
Moderate learning difficulties	1,038		57	82
Severe learning difficulties	2,430		48	38
Specific learning difficulties (eg, dyslexia, dyscalcula)	45		29	0
Other medical condition (eg, epilepsy, asthma, diabetes)	194		0	—
Multiple disabilities	1,421		31	48
Mental ill health	145		62	68
Hearing impairment	294		24	18
Disability affecting mobility	385		2	100
Visual impairment	81		12	50
Other physical disability	97		8	88
Emotional/behavioural difficulties	105		1	0
Other	410		3	100
Profound/complex disabilities	23		0	0
Temporary disability after illness (eg, post-viral) or accident	26		92	0
Total	**6,774**	**100**	**43**	**59**

Note: some respondents provided incomplete data, so the (total) data shown differ slightly from the sum of those in the individual rows

100

Mapping Provision: The Provision of and Participation in Further Education by Students with Learning Difficulties and/or Disabilities

Table 6. External institutions: students with learning difficulties and/or disabilities receiving FEFC-funded learning support through FEFC additional support bands

Annual cost for each student	Students in funding category		Average no. of students per college
	No.	%	(N=26 colleges)
£170–£500	1,243	85	48
£501–£1,000	176	12	7
£1,001–£2,000	1	0	0
£2,001–£4,000	34	2	1
£4,001–£5,600	0	0	0
£5,601–£8,800	0	0	0
£8,801 and over	14	1	1
Total	**1,468**	**100**	**57**

Turning to the question of unmet need, table 8 shows that around a third of respondent external institutions felt that 'internal unmet need' existed in their institution (a similar proportion to that recorded among sector colleges — see table 16 in chapter 5). Very few of the respondents (only six) were able or willing to estimate the numbers of such students affected, however.

When it comes to 'expressed external unmet need', that is, cases where potential students apply to the college but have needs which the college cannot meet, and who cannot, therefore, be enrolled, fewer than half of the external institutions (compared with nearly two-thirds of sector colleges) had systems in place to record such cases — as table 9 shows.

Once again, very few respondents were able to estimate the numbers of potential students affected (too few for the data reliably to be reported). Similarly, although some 62% of respondent external institutions claimed to be able to assess the level of potential demand for further education among their local populations with learning difficulties and/or disabilities (a similar proportion to that recorded in sector colleges — see table 22 in chapter 5), only two external

institutions were prepared to provide estimates, and these are not, therefore, reported here.

To conclude, we present external institutions' responses to the questions (presented in chapter 6 for sector colleges) relating to the institution's overall approach to provision for students with learning difficulties and/or disabilities. These responses are summarised in table 10.

Compared with the results for sector colleges (although exercising caution due to the small numbers of respondents), it would seem that external institutions are more likely to espouse an 'open access' policy. Despite this, however, they are less likely to adopt a cross-institution approach to learning support, and more likely to offer primarily discrete provision for students with learning difficulties and/or disabilities, than are their sector college counterparts.

Appendix 4

Table 7. External institutions: non-FEFC sources of additional support funding

Funding source	Colleges with students whose learning support is financed by the source in question	
	No.	%
Internal institution budget	8	42
LEA	14	74
TEC	0	0
Social Services	4	21
HA	6	32
ESF	2	11
Other*	5	26
Total (N=100%)	19	100

* 'other' includes a range of alternative sources of funding, the most common being charities and voluntary organisations supporting people with disabilities

Note: figures total to more than 100%, as respondents could indicate more than one funding source; LEA=local education authority; TEC=training and enterprise council; HA=health authority; ESF=European social fund

Table 8. External institutions: existence of internal unmet need

	Institutions identifying enrolled students with learning difficulties and/or disabilities whose learning support needs cannot be met (in full)	
	No.	%
Yes	10	33
No	17	57
Don't know	3	10
Total (N=100%)	30	100

Table 9. External institutions: systems for recording external unmet need

	Colleges identifying potential students with learning difficulties and/or disabilities who applied but could not be enrolled	
	No.	%
Yes	13	46
No	13	46
Don't know	2	7
Total (N=100%)	28	100

Mapping Provision: The Provision of and Participation in Further Education by Students with Learning Difficulties and/or Disabilities

Table 10. External institutions: overall approach to provision for students with learning difficulties and/or disabilities

Statement	No. of colleges responding					Average score	N=100%
	Strongly agree	*Agree*	*Neither agree nor disagree*	*Disagree*	*Strongly disagree*		
	(1)	*(2)*	*(3)*	*(4)*	*(5)*		
There is a cross-institution approach to learning support	7	12	5	3	1	2.3	28
The institution has a policy of 'open access' to all potential students irrespective of learning difficulty and/or disability	18	9	3	0	0	1.5	30
The institution employs specialist learning support staff who meet most learning support needs	6	8	8	6	0	1.7	28
All students are assessed for learning support needs	7	7	8	6	2	2.6	30
Learning support is mostly provided by lecturing/ tutorial staff	10	12	3	5	0	2.1	30
The main provision for students with learning difficulties and/or disabilities is on 'discrete' courses	4	16	3	4	3	2.5	30
Students are assessed for learning support only if self-identified, or on the basis of prior information	5	13	3	6	3	2.6	30

Printed in the United Kingdom for The Stationery Office
Dd. 303095 1/97 78166

103

Mapping Provision: The Provision of and Participation in Further Education by Students with Learning Difficulties and/or Disabilities